Tarot on Earth

A practical approach to reading the cards

Tarot on Earth
A practical approach to reading the cards

Tom Benjamin

Curious Journey Tarot
First edition 2017

Printed by CreateSpace
ISBN: 978-0-692-98507-6

Text © Copyright 2017 by Ben Jolivet (Tom Benjamin)
Curious Journey Tarot: www.curiousjourneytarot.weebly.com

◊ Contents ◊

For the amazing members of the
tarot community.
(Including the one holding this book.)

◊ Thank You ◊

Beth Hicks, editor extraodinaire.

Wandering Oracle, creator and publisher of the Marshmallow Marseille.

Kelly Fitzgerald of The Truth on Story, for hours and hours and hours of inspiration and for championing pip-based decks in a world that has forgotten them.

Wald and Ruth Ann Amberstone, though I never finished their correspondance course, what I learned through that course and their books has been immeasurable.

All the writers quoted in this book, whose works are listed in the appendix. As well as all the writers on tarot I've encountered in my life.

All the generous veiwers of my YouTube channel, whose comments and compliments have made my day, many, many days.

"Right, you've got a crooked sort of cross..." He consulted *Unfogging the Future.* "That means you're going to have 'trials and suffering'—sorry about that—but there's a thing that could be the sun...hang on...that means 'great happiness'...so you're going to suffer but be very happy...."

—J.K. Rowling, *Harry Potter and the Prisoner of Azkaban*

"To learn to play seriously is one of the great secrets of spiritual exploration."

—Rachel Pollack, *The Forest of Souls: A Walk Through the Tarot*

◊ Introduction ◊

As a frequent skipper of introductions, I offer this preview of what's in this section because you may want to read some of it.

· The approach
· My tarot "origin story"
· About the course
· Supplies needed
· About the deck
· Sources
· A quick tarot history

THE APPROACH

When I was in the college the first time, I met someone who would go on to become a lifelong friend. Because he was more than ten years older than I, he had lived more life, and his experiences were useful. He told me that if I wanted to get good at anything, I had to get my hands down into the dirt, into the mud, and get covered with it. Get messy, get sloppy, make mistakes, take risks, and—whatever happened—become stuck in that mud! Getting really good at anything, including life, isn't about doing it perfectly, cleanly, and gently; it's about doing it deeply, passionately, and full-out. Get in the sandbox and play. Do it even if there are dishes in the sink and clothes in the hamper. Make what you're passionate about a priority. Don't focus on doing the correct thing; focus on doing the thing at all. Years later, when I took a job in training and adult learning for a large hotel company, I learned that same lesson in a different way: mastering any task involved *a lot* of practice, some failing, more practice, and a lot of feedback.

That same message, delivered in two distinct ways, influenced my approach to the idea of getting good at anything. That's the approach of this course. I call it a course, because this isn't a passive learning device. It is an active learning event. It is, by design, a huge, delicious mud pit for you to crawl into and play. It is designed to be a messy, squishy, deep-dive into the deep-end of tarot, one that will leave you transformed into a deeper, more grounded, and, ideally, a better reader at the end of it. This of course means that you will likely have to face the seductive calls of perfectionism—the fear of not doing things "right," and the frustration of having to try more than once to get the result you want. But it also means that you become fully immersed in something you love doing. It means that you can spend hours and hours experimenting and playing and getting dirty—and you don't have to worry about getting mud on the carpet, or letting anyone see you sweat. Best of all, it will be fun to surrender to the moment, to get your hands in the dirt, and take my friend's advice. As adults, we are sorely disconnected from making mud pies, and the time has come to get back into the dirt and make mud pies again.

THIS FOOL'S JOURNEY – AN ORIGIN STORY

I like tarot origin stories. I like learning how people came to the cards. One of my favorite parts of Rachel Pollack's classic *Seventy-Eight Degrees of Wisdom* is the telling of how she found tarot, and the journey it took her on. I've read that book many times, but I've read her origin story even more—because there's something satisfying and fulfilling about it. About all origin stories, frankly. I love hearing how each person fell down the rabbit hole. With that in mind, I offer you my tarot origin story:

Before I ever was a tarot nerd, I was a theatre nerd—and I had a weird habit of getting cast in productions of the musical *Godspell.* Always in the role of John the Baptist/Judas (they're one dude, in *Godspell*). At nineteen, I played the role with a small theatre near my hometown. After a performance, out for post-show vittles at a chain restaurant, two friends drew from a bag a deck of cards wrapped in a white cloth. Tarot cards! In a chain restaurant! That served cedar plank salmon and frozen mudslides the size of a keg! Appalling! They casually explored the cards, comparing experiences, and chatting happily about readings they'd done and had done for them. I must have had a look of astonishment on my face, because one of them noticed, laughed, and offered a reading.

"N'oh my GOD NO! I don't believe in that stuff!"

An odd response. If I didn't believe in something, how could it tell me something I didn't want to know? But I was coming from a place of fear. Clearly, I *did* believe they were capable of something, because what I meant when I said "I don't believe in that stuff," was "I'm terrified they're going to tell me I'm dying!" From youth, I've been terrified of two things: Doctors and fortune telling. Both of which were likely to inform me of my imminent demise. Happily, I've come 'round on tarot. Maybe someday I'll do the same with doctors.

Despite my astonishment that someone had brought *tarot cards* to a cast party for a production of *Godspell,* in the days that followed I knew I had to learn more about those cards. I have no idea what deck they had. It was likely the Rider-Waite-Smith, but I don't know for sure. Whatever deck it was has remained elusive. I've looked at thousands over the years, waiting for the visual "zing" that would alert me that I'd found the one I was looking for. I've never zinged, at least with that one. Even remotely. Maybe it didn't exist at all. But I have such an image of the Hermit in my head, almost 20 years later, that I'm convinced it must still be out there.

A few days later, wandering the aisles of a local discount bookshop, I discovered a large book on reading the cards. I glanced at it. I skimmed the pages. My gaze fell upon a grayscale reprint of Pamela Colman Smith's Empress. Our eyes met. I felt something stir within. I closed the book, slipped it nonchalantly into the stack of other books I planned on buying, that way, if anyone noticed I was buying something so terrible, I could say something like, "Oh! I forgot I even had that in my hand! How silly. Let me just go ahead and dump this in the trash. Evil thing."

Days later, the *Original Rider-Waite Tarot Pack* arrived, in its purple and gold box. I remember still the visceral reaction I had as I lay on the bed and walked through the deck for the first time. The delight at The Fool and The Magician, the adoration of The Empress, the fascination with The Hanged Man, the chill as my eyes wandered over Death, the odd affection for the Knight of Pentacles. A lifelong love affair was born, for sure. And while the book I'd casually slipped into my pile of purchases at the dollar bookshop proved not to be remotely helpful, I discovered many more books that would send me down the path to reading. Shortly after, armed with a *Tarot for Dummies* style volume called *The Everything Tarot Book*, I gave a reading to a friend, who stared at me—astonished that everything I'd said made sense and addressed the concerns she'd had and the answers she needed. *How could I have done that?* I wondered. *And is this a responsibility I actually want?*

Happily, I did want that. And what I realized rather quickly was that the cards are an excellent way of engaging in one's own life. Whether from the religion of my youth or my own general temperament, I'd learned in the nineteen years leading up to that moment that life was a passive act. Things simply happened to you, and the only thing to do about it was hope that God changed things in your favor. I was, I assumed, powerless. Sure, people had said to me, "God helps those who help themselves," but I didn't really understand what that meant. Tarot, somehow, taught me that I didn't have to be an observer of my own life. I could engage with life, and, to the degree that it's possible, take the reins and became a verb rather than a noun. (The Chariot is my birth card. Go figure.) Tarot taught me that I could *do* rather than be *done to.* It was an amazing lesson. It changed my life.

That journey, coincidentally, began roughly at the same time I entered the world of adult learning. Between college summers, I took a job in a call center as a sales associate. Because I'd had a background in theatre,

I wound up moving into a training position. From there, I discovered the principles of adult learning theory. (In fact, as part of the interview process for that promotion, I had to create a brief training based on a hobby. I chose tarot. It never occurred to me what a brave thing it was to bring the cards into the corporate world. I did, though, and it got me the job.) In that role, I discovered how adults learn and retain information. I learned how to engage the hearts, minds, and egos of adult learners, so that they not only allow themselves to discover something new, but enjoy it and dig into what is taught.

For almost twenty years I've explored tarot and adult learning side-by-side. I've wanted to bring them together since those early days, and this is the first time I'm able to do that. The timing is right, and I couldn't be more excited to share that with you. Which takes us to…

ABOUT THIS COURSE

The activities and lessons in this course were developed during my own attempt to achieve the objectives of this book: namely, to find a practical, earthy approach to reading. The instructions and interludes have been developed over a long time reading tarot and reading about tarot.

Throughout, I refer to this as a "course" rather than a "book," purely because I want you to feel engaged in it in every way. Each chapter, or lesson, features a series of practice activities designed to deepen your relationship with tarot and provide readings that are clearer and more useful. Not to say that your readings aren't useful now, but the aim is to take them to a practical level that can help you and those you read for find answers that are grounded in the kinds of things we deal with day-to-day.

Where many modern books or courses explore the psychological and spiritual aspects of tarot, this one is aimed more at the kinds of readings that can help us deal with our daily lives—the kinds of readings that can help us become more active in life, or answer the kinds of questions we ask when we just need a straight answer about what's going on.

This is a workbook in every sense of the word. There's work to be done in this book, and much of that work is yours. It's what we in the adult learning business call an "asynchronous learning experience." Which, in English, means it's a class, but one that is self-paced and one in which you and the teacher are not in the same room at the same time. Books are great things, and books of musings and ruminations on the cards are how I learned to read. This isn't quite that, though there will be plenty of musings from yours truly. This is a participatory class. The activities will help you internalize what you're learning. As such, it's a bit more experiential than reading through and memorizing card meanings.

If you're anything like me, you will read the the book and encounter an activity and think, *Oh, that sounds kinda cool. I should try that.* Then promptly skip it and go to the next chunk of text. Don't be like me. While passive learning is easier, because it doesn't involve getting messy, because it doesn't involve risk, it's also been proven to be less memorable. Sitting back and absorbing what another has to say is attractive to me, because I don't want to do something wrong, screw it up, and feel like a fool. But, I repeat: *Don't be like me.* Remember my friend at the start of this intro: we are getting into the dirt together, and we're going to have fun doing it. *Do things wrong! Look silly! Make a mess!* Please, for the love of all that is good and decent in the world, *give yourself permission to play!* Tarot started as a game, so let's play! Even if you have a more spiritual bent, the Rachel Pollack quote at the start of this text should inspire you to play a bit more.

If, at the end of this course, your book doesn't look like it's been through hell, I'm going to feel devastated. Have you seen those novelty notebooks in the bookstores? *Wreck This Journal?* I want you to wreck this book, damn it! Nobody is testing you. Nobody is looking over your shoulder judging. Let the lessons in this book be the place you experiment, the place you play and approach tarot with the innocence of a child and the wisdom of an adult. Abandon perfectionism. Let yourself off the hook. Have fun.

Amen.

This course focuses on Marseille-style decks. Allow me to define that for the purposes of this course, because I tend to use that term more liberally than purists might allow. Specifically, Marseille-type tarots, *Tarots de Marseille,* are decks born in France in the seventeenth and eighteenth century. They pre-date the Golden Dawn and, thus, the famous deck created by A.E. Waite and Pamela Colman Smith. (I've made that choice for several reasons, which I'll outline below—but do know that the techniques we explore in this book can and will enhance the techniques you're already using with Waite-Smith-inspired packs.) More generally, I use "Marseille-style" as a catch-all for all decks created before and after the Marseille tarots that feature pip cards (traditionally the "minor arcana") without what I call "situational illustrations." What I mean by situational illustrations are those Waite-Smith style cards, where humans or animals (or other beings) are interacting with the suits in a scene or situation that helps suggest a divinatory meaning. Not all of these decks are Marseille, and Marseille doesn't qualify all of these decks, but for the sake of simplicity, I'm going to use that as a blanket term.

All systems have their pros and cons, and all methods offer something useful. I chose this particular system to work with because it offers a bit of distance from the traditional images that have become so well-known to readers around the globe. There's something incredibly useful about having a picture like the Four of Cups to reference in the midst of a reading; there's also something freeing about *not* having that image. The pictorial pips give us a bounding box that keeps us close to what we see in the image we're looking at. That's useful, because as I frequently moan, if anything is possible, then *anything is possible.* What I mean is that limitlessness can be overwhelming. When we look at the man and the tree and the hand coming out of the sky offering a cup, that creates a context for the card that helps us assign meaning.

On the other hand, there are times when the image can limit us in ways that feel less helpful. When we think for example about the Three of Swords, the image known to us from Pamela Colman Smith's art, and famously borrowed from the *Sola Busca* cards, we see three cards stabbing a heart. It's hard not to see that as loss or heartbreak. But threes more generally are about growth, about expansion, and about two things becoming one. None of that is available to us in the image, and, as such, it makes it hard when reading for another to talk about the idea of growth. All they see is a Valentine that's been stabbed to death. There's also something to be said about the elemental aspect of the cards. Swords, if we accept them as related to air, are about the mind and the mouth, so to speak. They're about thought and communication, what we think, what we say, and how we say it. Thus, the Three of Swords has less to do with the heart than the mind. Releasing ourselves from the image can provide new dimension to a reading. And it doesn't mean that those cards have to be tossed on the fire; it just means we're adding new layers to our abilities.

When I became interested in reading with these types of decks, I couldn't quite find the book I was looking for—though I read some great ones that are quoted in the text, and described in the appendix. I hope it doesn't sound arrogant to say that creating this book changed the way I read for the better. It did. I say that because I had to put myself through all the activities I'm going to ask you to attempt. And I can say that going through them brought me closer to the kinds of readings I've wanted to do more of: down-to-earth, grounded, practical, and accessible. Because, as I've said and will say again and again throughout, nothing is wrong with the psychological and spiritual. It's just that sometimes we want something that's a little earthier, a little more mundane. And why shouldn't a reader have that in their toolbox, too?

Whether you take this course and use what you learn only with pip-style decks, or you use it to enhance your experience with Rider-Waite or even Thoth-style decks, what I want to make clear is that my goal is to add, not limit. I want you to walk away with more, not less: additional skills, new ideas, different outlooks, and fresh techniques. What you do with them after that is up to you, and is entirely right for you and your readings. That is the great thing about what we do: if anything is possible, *anything is possible.*

SUPPLIES

All you'll need for this course is a tarot deck with pip-style minors. (I've listed some of my favorites in the appendix.) I attempted to leave enough space for many of the activities, but page count equals cost, and to keep this book affordable there are times where I've elected not to do that. You may want to get a notebook or journal to use it for all of the activities, so you have them in one place. I recommend keeping your work, because it will be helpful in years to come when you want to recall how you came to a certain meaning for a certain card. Also, it's just fun to explore how your practice has evolved.

ABOUT THE DECK PICUTRED IN THIS COURSE

The deck used to illustrate the examples in this book is *The Marshmallow Marseille* by Wandering Oracle. When working on this course, I wanted something fresh and modern, but that still felt like the original *Tarot de Marseille.* I found both in this beautiful pack of cards. I want to express my gratitude to Wandering Oracle for allowing me to use these wonderful images, and encourage you all to visit their shop: www.wanderingoracle. com.

Please note that the images from that deck are used with the permission of Wandering Oracle, and further reproduction is prohibited.

ABOUT SOURCES

As a writer, it is profoundly important to me that originators of work receive the credit they're due. Throughout this text, I have aimed to attribute ideas, concepts, and intellectual property to the author from whom I learned it. Where an idea or concept is not tied to a specific author, it is because it came from my own study and development—or because it is a concept in wide-enough use that attribution to any one author or creator is unncessary.

Tarot is similar to cooking, in that writing about it is complicated. With food, so much has been written, said, explored, and experimented with, that it's not always easy to trace the source of a recipe. It's also possible to reach the same conclusions as another chef without ever having had contact with their food. This book is one recipe, and I've done my best to credit the chefs who inspired me everywhere I could.

ON TAROT HISTORY

Many tarot books begin with a history of the cards. For our purposes, the only history I feel we have to be aware of is that tarot started as a game. From what I can tell, the cards had no metaphysical or esoteric aim beyond the spiritual joy of *play*. That's important to me, because it frees us to have fun with what we're learning. And while what we're doing is frequently to serious ends, getting there can be messy and playful and fun. And that is how we truly learn anything.

For those who are new to tarot, I've mentioned some names in this text you may not be familiar with. For your sake, here are the main players:

Antoine Court de Gebelin — An 18th century Frenchman who was the first to claim tarot had mystical properties and erroneously assigned

Egyptian heritage to the cards.

Etteilla (Jean-Baptiste Alliette) — An 18th century French cartomancer, who wrote about all kinds of divination and codified definitions for the pips that are still influential today.

A.E. Waite — A 19th century English occultist, who commissioned the most popular tarot deck in the English-speaking world. That deck was drawn by:

Pamela Colman Smith (Pixie) — A 19th century artist who revolutionized tarot by creating meaningful scenes on each of the pips (which Waite termed "the lesser arcana").

And one organization is worth note:

The Hermetic Order of the Golden Dawn — A 18th/19th century occult organization that yielded A.E. Waite, Pamela Colman Smith, and Alestair Crowley, whose *Thoth Tarot* is another popular system.

With that in mind, let the games begin!

PART I: THE PIPS

◊ The Pips ◊

We're going to begin this course with the part of the deck that gets the least amount of love in many books. It certainly got only a passing glance from many of the esoteric-minded people who gave us the tarot we know and love today. For many thinkers in the history of tarot who viewed the cards as a book of lost knowledge, the trumps *were* the tarot; the pips were something that had latched on to tarot like a parasite and needed to be dealt with as such. The pips belonged to the land of cartomancy, while the trumps were the land of spiritual development. Early tarot histories claim that the trumps were divorced from the pips in order to create modern pip playing cards. (They were wrong.)

No doubt the trumps are important, but I like to think of them as the board of directors, CEOs, and the senior officers of a company. They're at the top of the chain, making decisions, proclaiming things, and occasionally getting involved in a scandal. They're setting the larger direction for the organization. The courts, meanwhile, are like the managers below them, who directly supervise the worker bees—or, more diplomatically, the "individual contributors"—who are on the ground floor, doing the work. The pips are those very workers, the ones in the field making the sales, engaging with customers, and doing the work of living. While the CEOs might be impressive, no company is anything without the frontline employees who are literally making the machine go.

The pips are doing the real *work* of tarot. They're in the field, on the job, describing our lives as we live them day to day. They're the events that happen to us at the grocery store, in the office, at the PTA, and the reasons for our dates or divorces. There are more of them, and they describe more banal, daily things—the very things we spend most of our lives dealing with and thinking about. They're what get us excited and what keep us up at night. And, as such, they are as important as any other part of the deck. A.E. Waite may not have thought so, but Pamela Colman Smith clearly did. Her artwork raised the "lesser arcana" to the level of their more "important" counterparts, and though we're not using her deck here, we owe her a debt of gratitude for giving them the gravitas they deserve.

In this course, we're going to start with these hard-working, useful cards. And we're going to explore a system of learning their meanings that will both give you boundaries to work within, and the elasticity to stretch them where they want to be stretched.

Lesson 1:
◇ ◇
Numerology

The approach we're going to take to these cards is a fun, gentle kind of math. In essence, each pip has a number and a suit. Each number means something. Each suit means something. Together, they partner to create a unique meaning. Those meanings are mutable—they shift, and they work in the context of the reading and the question in order to truly come into their own. As we work together in Part I, you're going to learn a host of tools to help you determine the basic meanings for the pips, and how they morph into more specific meanings during a reading.

Camelia Elias, one of my favorite tarot writers, wrote a blog post called "Size Matters" (July 29, 2017). In it, she explains that "meaning is situational, it has no inherent existence. In other words, meaning doesn't exist." Being the take-no-prisoners, tell-it-like-it-is teacher that she is, it's a provocative statement. What she means (I think) is that the meanings we learn for cards aren't fixed and unchangeable. If we are listening to the reading, the meaning will evolve in the context of other cards, the question, and our own senses at the time. That is the essence of working with the cards. And one thing beginning readers struggle with, no matter the chosen system, is rigidity in meanings. The Nine of Wands means, as depicted by Waite and Colman Smith, "burden." Done. Now it shows up in response to a question, "what's the best thing about my relationship?" It's a burden to you! That's the best thing about your relationship? I suppose it's possible. Some relationships don't have much going for them and the best thing about them is still pretty terrible. Still, one hopes a relationship that bad would have been escaped from. If we are less rigid, if we relax into the concept, we might say that it's a labor of love. That it's hard work, but it's satisfying; it's something we're passionate about, and we're willing to do the work. "Burden," not so much; heavy, yes.

For all that, though, we do need something to stand on—especially in decks without situational or scenic pips. If the Nine of Wands in a Marseille deck shows up, we've got nine wands and some flowers. Nothing else. "Burden" may be a limiting definition for that card in any Waite-Smith deck, but at least we've got a dude carrying some heavy sticks to spark something.

What we have in Marseille decks are numbers. That's "all." But with those numbers, we can find a wealth of meaning.

Tarot numerology is fluid, to say the least. From what I can gather, it's based in part on the mathematical work of Pythagoras; partly—maybe—on Kabbalistic numerology; partly on Golden Dawn correspondences; partly on general "new age" numerology, which is also partly based on Pythagoras, Chinese systems, and just a general settling in of meaning over time. Like most things, there isn't any one system. Frankly, if you wanted, you could make one up on your own. Pedants will say that things should be rooted in history, in the practices of others. Given that, tarot would still be a game, and we'd be reading animal entrails to discover what the harvest will look like. To pedants, then, I say, "nonsense!" If you want to make up a numerological system for tarot, do it. Who cares what anyone else says? What matters is that (a) you have a system and (b) you (more or less) stick to it.

That said, there is some benefit in basing your system on established numerology. First, others have done the hard work; second, it's easier to discuss your work with others when there is at least some commonality between your methods and theirs; third, for better or worse, there is a measure of credibility when a system is based on research rather than improvisation.

To my knowledge, no book exists (yet) specifically on tarot numerology. And if there were one, some people would love it and other people wouldn't. Such is the nature of these things. Yoav Ben-Dov and Alejandro Jodorowsky both spend time on the numerological meanings in their books. Because Ben-Dov was Jodorowsky's student, there are similarities—but, happily, there are also plenty of differences. For example, Ben-Dov says (among other things) that number one is about potential, wholeness, union of opposites, concentration. Jodorowsky says that it represents everything in potential, everything remaining to be done. Slight but important differences. Those differences are useful, because they help us find the colors we're looking for as we begin down this path.

In the development of my own meaning for the numbers, I started with Ben-Dov and Jodorowsky and then researched tarot numerology and general numerology online. I chose seven sources. I took notes from each, and placed those notes in a spreadsheet. Each row, a number; each column, a different description of that number. Then, I combed through each row, reading across each column to find similarities, differences and things that jumped out at me. I highlighted the similarities, bolded the differences, and ultimately chose a handful of keywords that seemed to summarize the meaning of the number. Ultimately, the choices were mine, but they were based on seven other sources.

The benefit of going through this was that I made a strong, personal connection to each of the numbers' meanings. And, in reading so many descriptions of the numbers, I also made connections to keywords or phrases that I didn't include in my final list. These ideas pop up in readings from time to time. For example, one source referred to the number two as, in part, a crossroads (BiddyTarot.com). That concept did not make it into my distillation, but it is easy to see how—especially in a pip deck—two crossed wands could easily suggest a crossroads. There have been times when the specific card in a reading seems to suggest just that kind of duality (one of my chosen keywords for that number). Had I not done that research, I might not have had the idea of a crossroad spring to mind. And it's important that things like that do spring to mind, because we've already seen that meaning is mutable. As Yoav Ben-Dov said in his book *Tarot: The Open Reading*, nothing that happens in a reading is accidental. We want things to pop into our minds during readings; that's a good thing.

That brings us to your first activity. Essentially, to follow in my footsteps.

Activity 1.1: Numerology Research and Distillation

Objective: Codify a numerological meaning for numbers one through ten by researching and comparing results, then distilling those results into your own definition.

Why you should do this: This kind of research is useful because you internalize meanings naturally. Words and phrases you forget now may show up in readings later. Further, you will build a stronger connection to the meanings you decide on, because you will have whittled the list down from many possibilities. Because you choose what the numbers mean (based on several sources) you're more likely to remember them. Your active work in poring over and then deciding on the meanings of the numbers makes it more likely that you'll be able to connect to the meanings you need when you need them.

Instructions:

1. Use a spreadsheet or a long sheet of craft paper, and make a table. The table should have eleven rows. The first row will be the column titles (see example at the top of the next page), and the remaining rows will be numbers one through ten.

2. Decide on a number of resources you wish to explore. I chose seven, but you needn't do that many. I recommend an odd number, because you will have a "tie breaker" if you need one. Add a column for each resource, then add another column for your distillations.

	Source 1	Source 2	...
One			
Two			
...			

3. If you have the Jodorowsky or Ben-Dov books, you may start there; if not, no worries. Use the library and/or web searches to look for numerology meanings. I recommend varying your search terms, so that you find results specifically related to tarot numerology, results related to general numerology, biblical or Kabbalistic numerology, Pythagorean and Chinese numerology, etc. The more varied your results, the more interesting this activity will be. (I focused on general, tarot, and astrological numerology.)

4. Label each of your columns with the name of of your chosen sources. (This may not seem important, but you will want to reference it later—for example, if you're writing a book about this process.)

5. In the row for the number, write highlights of that source's definition under the column for that source. (For example, in the "Two" row, write highlights from Ben-Dov's meanings for two in the column you labeled "Ben-Dov.")

6. Repeat for each of your sources.

7. Take a break.

8. Read through the highlights for each number. Identify similarities. This will be helpful. If, for example, all your sources use the word "seed" to describe number one, it's a pretty safe bet that word should wind up in your final distillation.

9. Read through and look for differences. Where sources disagree, explore which side you fall on. If one source calls two "duality" and another calls it "crossroad," ask yourself which feels more right— or if both feel right. If you feel yourself disagreeing with a choice, explore why. Understanding why you disagree with or dislike some- thing is often a good way of codifying your final definitions.

10. Choose the words or phrases that resonate with you, and add them to your distillation column. You're not etching this in stone. Trust your gut. You can change it later. Repeat for all ten numbers.

11. Take a break. A few days, even.

12. Look through your distillations and see if each number is differ- ent enough from the others. Do three and six look too similar to be useful? Are any of the distillations vague or impractical? If you were to use these words in a reading, would they leave someone scratching their head? Pay special attention to numbers seven and nine, because they are notoriously difficult to define. If you find that numbers are too similar or definitions too unclear, go back to

your sources and refine your distillations. Try to avoid using the same word in more than one distillation. Make each one distinct, clear, and useful. The more distinct they are now, the more likely your readings will be sharp, clear, and useful later.

13. Take a break.

Note on steps seven, eleven, and thirteen. If you're a stubborn student like me, you will consider skipping those steps and racing through this course. That's what I'd do. But I'd be denying myself the opportunity to let my brain rest and absorb what I'd learned so far. Learning experts tell us that there are two kinds of memory, aptly named short and long term. All information lives in short-term memory for, well, a short amount of time. Some of that information passes into long-term memory. A lot of factors affect how information moves from short-term memory into long-term memory, but one of those factors is volume. The more information you cram into your mind, the less likely most of it is to make the move. Which means that if you want to learn or study anything, "cramming" is a bad idea. We remember things best in short, small, similar chunks of information, repeated over and over. If you *really* want to remember what you're researching, you will take a break.

Debrief: This activity exposed you to a variety of opinions about numerological meanings; it allowed you to see divergent opinions, from an array of sources; it forced you to explore whether you agree or disagree with several definitions, making you more confident in your final choices; and, ultimately, you will retain your final definitions more easily, because you have chosen them after some thoughtful exploration.

You're not locked into anything you've entered into your chart. In fact, nothing you do in this course should ever be locked in. As time goes on, you will evolve your keywords and concepts. That's natural. You will have readings or give readings that completely blow your mind, and that leave everything you thought about the number seven forever changed. That's the best possible thing! I mentioned in my intro that writing this book changed the way I read. That was inevitable, because, as you'll see, several of the examples I'll use with you in the next few lessons forced me to put my go-to concepts through the wringer. Great readers are great students and are open to new views. That never stops being true.

You may want to take a moment now, before proceeding to lesson two, to think about what you've done and how it will help you going forward. In fact, it's wise to do that at the end of each lesson. We remember what we find value in remembering. And so, it's good to connect what we've done to what's important to us. If you spend a few moments now thinking about your tarot goals and how this activity brought you closer to any one of those goals, it makes it more likely that the information you've worked on will move from short-term into long-term memory— and that's a very good thing.

Lesson 2:

◊ ◊

Light and Shadow

Take a moment and consider your distilled numerological meanings. Then, compare them to mine (below). Please note that you are not to compare our meanings for quality. Your distillations are great, and whatever differences exist between yours and mine have to do with our temperaments, preferences, and experiences. I'm showing you mine, now, because it's useful to see how we both landed where we did, and it will help as I share reading examples down the line. You'll have a better sense of why I got where I did. But you shouldn't revise your table of results if they're completely different from mine. Also note that I'm giving you distillations of my distillations—the original work I did on this was much longer, but I want to keep it simple for the sake of space and sanity.

Table 2.1: Numerological Keywords

Number	Distillation
ONE	Seed, impulse, urge
TWO	Duality, pairing, connection, balance
THREE	Growth, triangulation
FOUR	Foundation, stability
FIVE	Disruption
SIX	Re-balance, beauty
SEVEN	Introspection, self-reflection
EIGHT	Work, commitment, dedication
NINE	The final push, uncertainty
TEN	Completion, resolution

Are your distillations (which are probably longer than this) similar? It's OK if they're not. But do you see that most of the keywords I've developed happen to be fairly positive? Or, if not positive, neutral? Only numbers five and nine really have any negative implication, and nine is, at most, annoying.

Do your distillations have a similar theme? It's likely, having researched several sources on numerology, the numbers themselves have a pretty innocuous quality. But that neutral-to-positive majority doesn't add much color to a reading. If you ask "what's wrong with my relationship" and you get the Six of Cups, you have, in essence, beautiful, balanced feelings. I feel too good? Too balanced? Too even? Sure, it's possible, but...

Tarot is full of light and shadow, or positive and negative, like everything else in life—including the atoms we're made out of. Everything in life is a series of degrees. Thich Nhat Hanh, the great Buddhist writer, talks about the idea of a toothache. We don't notice we *don't* have a toothache, and we're not thankful every day that we don't have one—until we *do* have one and we're desperate to get rid of it. Nobody wants a toothache, but we need them in order to appreciate *not* having one. He also talks about how a rose can only grow when it is fertilized with manure. Or, as Dolly Parton once said: "The way I see it, if you want the rainbow, you gotta put up with the rain."

We all want positive things, and we all want to believe that we can be happy most of the time. But if we're happy most of the time, we're likely to take it for granted—so we need the shadow times. And, let's be honest, when people want readings, it's frequently because something annoying is going on and they want to know when it'll be over. We can't explore when something negative will be over if we don't have meanings for the cards that speak to those experiences. And if we want to avoid the negative consequences of actions, we also need cards that can represent those. We can't have a series of meanings that are too good or too bad. We need light and shadow. That's what this lesson is about, and that brings us to our next activity.

Activity 2.1: Light and Shadow

Objective: Balance your numerological meanings with light and shadow, so that readings are more layered and more realistic.

Why you should do this: If all your meanings are positive, neutral, or negative, your readings won't reflect life and all its shades. This activity brings balance to your distillations and to your eventual tarot readings.

Instructions:

1. Review your original distillations one more time. Are you happy with them? Are they clear? Do they feel different enough from one another to constitute an array of experience? (Pay special attention to seven and nine; they are frequently vague.)

2. Using worksheet 2.1, or a spreadsheet similarly arranged, enter your distillations into the first box, going down the first column from one to ten.

3. Beginning with one, read your distillation. Is it positive, negative, or neutral? If it is positive, re-enter those words into the "light" box; if negative, then into the "shadow" box. If the words are neutral, leave them alone.

4. For each set of keywords that has a positive (light) feeling about them, think about what their shadows are. Note that shadow isn't necessarily the opposite. If six is "beauty," the shadow of that isn't necessarily "ugliness." It might be, but it doesn't have to be. The shadow of beauty could also be "vanity." Be thoughtful about this. Trust your instincts, and then question your instincts. That will help you make decisions but also give you a way of checking yourself before settling for something easy.

5. For each set of keywords that has a negative (shadow) feeling about them, think about what their lights are. Again, this isn't necessarily the opposite. Five is frequently "disruption" in some way. The light of that isn't exactly harmony—that has more of a six feeling. The light of disruption could be shaking up old habits.

6. For each set of keywords that are neutral, you have a slightly more difficult task. You need to think about each of these as both light *and* shadow. Introspection, from my list, is fairly neutral. In a light mode, it might suggest self-exploration and therapeutic work. In a shadow mode, it might suggest naval-gazing or self-obsession.

7. Do this for all numbers, one through ten.

8. Take breaks in between!

Debrief: I'm a firm believer that no card is fully negative or positive. Each can embody something good and something bad. In fact, "good" and "bad" themselves can be both good and bad. The notoriously nasty Devil card can suggest addiction, but it can also suggest a sexy weekend. Temperance may suggest moderation, but it also may suggest a stick-in-the-mud. The light or shadow depends on the question and the context. We will talk about both of those things later.

In the meantime, let me share with you my light and shadow examples. Feel free to contrast, but again not for quality. Your answers are great, because they come from you. If something I've found strikes you as useful, please take it and run with it. I would do the same were you here with me. But this is not a test; it's just an example. And again, I share this in part so that my sample readings will make more sense.

Table 2.2: Light and Shadow

NUMBER	DISTILLATION	LIGHT	SHADOW
ONE	Seed, impulse	Potential	Wasted potential
TWO	Duality, pairing, connection, balance	Duality, pairing, connection, balance	Discord, disconnection, imbalance
THREE	Growth, triangulation	Growth, production	Stunted growth, over-growth
FOUR	Foundation, stability	Foundation, stability	Conservatism, rigidity
FIVE	Disruption	Shaking up patterns	Disruption, conflict
SIX	Beauty, re-balance	Beauty, harmony, re-union	False harmony, vanity
SEVEN	Introspection, self-reflection	Self-reflection, thoughtfulness	Self-obsession, reclusiveness
EIGHT	Work, commitment, dedication	Commitment, hard word, dedication	Obsession, labor, compulsion
NINE	Uncertainty, the final push	Abandonment of perfection, forging ahead	Anxiety, uncertainty, pessimism
TEN	Completion, resolution	Completion, resolution	Completion, resolution

These have evolved and continue to. Only when I was writing this did I realize that the shadow of six could include vanity, for example. We're not committing ourselves to these words; we're giving ourselves an ignition point for reading. Think of these key words as the flint on a box of matches. The cards are the match. When we strike one against the other, a fire flares up—but it's not the same kind of fire every time. The purpose and the conditions under which a fire is lit aren't always the same. On a quiet night at home, lighting candles for dinner, a match has a subdued, gentle, maybe sexy quality. Fire behaves differently when wind whips cold outside and the match is pressed against a stack of dried pine. It's fire, always, but its context and behavior changes.

This is another exploration of Camelia Elia's assertion that meaning doesn't exist. I've read twos as balance for as long as I can remember, even before Marseille-style decks, because many of the Waite-Smith twos feel like they're somehow related to that concept. But there are times when two feels like *imbalance*, and there have been times where two suggests *boundaries*. Why? I don't know. But when one sees the Two of Swords in a Marseille deck, there's suddenly an inside and an outside. The Ace doesn't have that; it just has a line. But the Two of Swords, in particular, creates an almond-shaped container (a *mandorla*). It makes sense, because life needs boundaries. It also makes sense because swords are weapons, which is one way boundaries have been defended through-out history.

That process, of exploring the meaning and context, and making con-nections between those and the world around us, is really what a reading is. It's a game of mental associations made between the suit, the number, and the question or context. We take the words we know and the images we see and we let them lead us on a journey toward meaning.

My list will continue to change, and I'll probably tinker with it even as I edit these pages later. Fine. Good. The point is having a place to start from, because we don't have a picture of the person leaving eight cups behind. We just have the eight, and we just have the cups—which serves as an elegant segue to our next lesson. Before we do, though, pause for a moment and think about how you stand to come closer to your tarot goals from doing what we've done together. Again, that will help you retain what you've learned.

Worksheet 2.1: Light and Shadow

NUMBER AND DISTILLATION	LIGHT	SHADOW

Interlude 1:
◊ On Spirituality ◊
and Magic

Because so much of this book covers the practical aspects of tarot, my Spidey sense tells me I should take a moment and talk a bit about the spiritual and magical aspects of tarot. It's important to me, as I hope I've made clear, that I not negate any spiritual relationship you have with this tool. Far be it from me to take away anything that brings you that kind of connection. There are too many people in the world trying to destroy whatever magic exists in it. My focus is practical purely because there are countless books on the spiritual aspects of the cards. What I haven't found in my journey is a course in tarot that does what we're talking about. (And if there is one, my apologies for having missed it. The world is large.)

Underscoring every practical, grounded method we'll talk about here, is the fact that *tarot works.* It just does. It doesn't always, like most things, but it works most of the time for a lot of people. And I have no idea why or how. I don't know if it's Jung's synchronicity. I don't know if it's simply that all cards in the deck could answer all questions well enough. I don't know if it really is magic. What I do know is that it works, and there's no real reason that I can detect as to why it should. And the very fact that it works and it doesn't make sense that it should is one of the things that makes me love it so much.

I don't ever want to know how it works, frankly. As a logical person with a curious mind, I enjoy learning how things work. I want to see how laws and sausages get made, even though we're not supposed to want that. But I never want science to come up with an explanation of why divination of any kind is a useful tool. And luckily scientific people simply say that it doesn't work, and they've left us to our own devices. That's fine. I have boundless respect for scientists, especially in a world where fact has become "fake news." I do, though, wish more scientists had a greater tolerance for magic. Ever since Copernicus realized that the earth moves around the sun and not the other way around, science has managed to do amazing things that tell us about the world around us. But none of them can really tell us *why* the Universe—or, now that we know we're not the only one, the multiverses—are here, and why we don't all just go falling through space like a rock into a ravine.

I grew up in the Christian tradition. I obeyed the dictums and took the rules seriously. Everyone assumed that I would grow up to be a priest. I never wanted to be a priest; the thought never crossed my mind. And I recognize now that I learned to resent priests, just a little. Why should they have a direct-connect to God, when I was forced to use an operator—

an operator who looked down on me and told me everything I'd done was wrong.

Even the idea of prayer frustrated me. As a life-long sufferer of anxiety, I have vivid memories of late nights awake *begging* God for something or other to happen or not—or for an explanation or answer I desperately needed. Being greeted with silence, I was told, was the answer. Sometimes God says no. Sure enough, but couldn't he at least tell me *why?*

Those practitioners of my childhood religion would likely gasp to hear me say this, but I feel tarot is a more practical method of praying than begging a silent entity for help and never knowing if you've been heard. In an episode of *The West Wing*, a priest tells the president a fable about a believer strapped in a flood. A man comes by and tells the believer, "There's a storm coming, you're going to drown. Come with me, we'll get to safety." The believer tells the man that God will save him and sends the man on the way. The flood comes, and a man with a boat floats by, offering assistance. Again, the believer declines because he has faith that God will save him. Finally, rescuers appear in a helicopter and offer help, and again the believer refuses because he's waiting for God to save him. The believer drowns. And when he gets to Heaven, he asks God why He didn't save him. God says to the believer, "I sent you help three times. What the hell are you doing here?"

Things come in to our lives to help us, and why shouldn't we use them? For centuries, people have viewed any form of divination as the tool of the devil. Frankly, I think that comes not from a pure religious belief, but from a thirst for power. Power comes in part from having access.

If I require you to access God, you have power over me. If I have access to God without you, you lose your power. If I can communicate with the higher beings, whatever I may believe them to be, then the organizations that make money from acting as intermediaries lose their power. This is not to say that all faiths have nefarious intent and that all of them care purely about money. But some do. And once one has power, giving it up is not remotely tempting.

Whether the cards are used as a practical device for answering questions we don't otherwise have the answers to, whether they're used as a guide for spiritual development, or all of the above, they are a tool that has arrived in our lives. And I say taking advantage of it is not only a good thing, it's a responsible thing. It's getting in the car or the boat or the helicopter when the flood is coming. Why wait in vain for a silent response? The voices of the higher powers in the world aren't intelligible to the ears of most humans. But if we have tools that can help us communicate with those powers, why the hell not take advantage of them?

From our earliest days, people have used tools of all kinds to find the answers they need. And the thing is, if those things didn't work, people would stop using them. We haven't. These tools do provide us with answers.

There are also branches of theology that disdain knowledge. There's murkiness around even Adam and Eve. The Tree of Knowledge of Good and Evil is forbidden them, and the Devil tempts them into eating from it. They suddenly see themselves as they are, and the world as it is, and God is furious. Perhaps that's where the hatred of divination comes from. Access to knowledge is associated with the Devil from the earliest texts of the world's big three religions. I could never reconcile a God who put knowledge in front of humanity and then tried to stop them from gaining it. That makes zero sense to me—from a logical or faith-based perspective. And while I apologize to anyone whose beliefs I'm trampling on here, I argue that the story of the first humans and their fall from grace has less to do with God, and more to do with humanity.

Knowledge can be scary. We can't unlearn things or un-know them. What's known remains known. And those flashes of revelation can be alarming. It's why, as we'll learn, clients will sometimes say a reading is "wrong." There's great beauty, but also great fear in knowing the unknown. In Anton Chekhov's *Uncle Vanya*, a "plain" (I don't like that word, but that's how she describes herself) young woman is quietly but desperately in love with a local doctor. She's never brought it up to him because she's afraid her feelings will go unrequited. Finally, her stepmother suggests it's time to know the answer once and for all, and if the answer is that he doesn't love her, then he should stop coming around. Sonya, the young woman, agrees to let her stepmother ask the doctor about his feelings. But as she leaves her stepmother to the task, she says, unheard, "Not knowing is better, because at least then there's hope." It's a devastating moment, because *of course*. Once she finds the answer, she can't un-know it, and all her hopes will be dashed. There's the possibility that she already knows what he's going to say and can't bring herself to hear the words aloud. But she's suffering, and she finally gives in. It's an incredibly human moment, but it's a reminder that knowledge can wound as well as enlighten. The world is not entirely lovely, and we don't always get what we want.

There's a cliché in tarot, but it's wise, that we should never ask a question we don't want the answer to. That's true not only in tarot, but in life. Once Adam and Eve ate from the tree of knowledge and saw what was in front of them, the revelation must have stunned them. Knowing what was unknown *is* a fall from grace, because ignorance *is* a kind of bliss. Sometimes not knowing is better, because then at least there's hope.

As a reader, it's wise to consider how we care for what the client may or may not be able to hear. Understanding that once they bite into the apple they may not be able to see things as they were. In the story of Adam and Eve, the Devil may not be evil for having tempted them into knowledge, but rather into forcing them into something they weren't yet ready for. And the punishment wasn't literal eviction from Eden, but rather the discovery that nothing was ever as perfect as it seemed before the blinders were removed.

I do believe that there is a spiritual aspect to knowledge. I think science could be a religion, if religious people weren't so scared and scientists weren't so resentful. I think science is magic. I think scientists are telling us that God's creation, Earth, is hurting, and we have to do something to save it. And sadly too many people say, "No, that's not a thing." I think that tarot is magic, and I think that knowledge is magic, and like any kind of magic it can be used for good or ill. Like most things, context and intent matter a great deal. The cards themselves aren't magic. They're pieces of paper, and generally they're impregnated with plastic coatings and chemicals—so it's not like they're even organic, in most cases. The concept of tarot is magical, and our ability to find meaning in patterns is magic. Intuition is magic. Intuition, I think, may actually be the language of God. It's the common thread between us and whatever exists beyond us that clearly has answers for us if we're willing to learn a way of translating it.

We can get practical, helpful answers from tarot—but only because there's some kind of something in the world that allows that to be possible. And so while I'm a stickler for down-to-earth readings and answers, I say that tarot is every inch a magical or spiritual experience, simply because it works! There are readings I've done for folks that have left both the client and me astonished at the reading's insight and accuracy. Don't tell me that's not magical. And so, in case you were worried I was just a boring old curmudgeon bent on spoiling the fun of divination, I offer this rambling, somewhat sacrilegious, but heartfelt treatise on tarot, magic, and spirituality.

◊ Lesson 3: Elements ◊

Reading pip-based tarot decks involves a simple equation:

$$number + element = meaning$$

We'll expand on that it, but for the moment that's all we need. To solve it, we need to explore those elements and what they represent.

If you have a relationship with tarot already, it is likely you have a sense of the elemental correspondences between the suits. There are variations, but by-and-large, they are:

Wands/Batons = Fire
Cups = Water
Swords = Air
Coins/Pentacles = Earth

Before we dig deeper, let's jump into a quick activity.

Activity 3.1: Element meanings

Objective: Define what each suit/element means in daily life.

Why you should do this: Simply put, without a clear understanding of the elemental meanings, reading pip-style decks is difficult.

Instructions:

1. Using the space below, describe the meaning of each of the elements (fire, water, air, and earth). If you are unfamiliar with the meanings, use tarot guidebooks or websites to research them. As with the numbers, you may want to explore several sources and distill the "final" answers. (It may be worth doing this even if you are familiar with the elements.) Write those definitions in the space below.
2. Take a break.

Fire	Water
Air	Earth

Debrief: Without a clear understanding of the elemental meanings, reading pip-style decks is difficult. This allows you an opportunity to discover or re-discover what the elements mean in life.

For contrast, here are mine. As always, yours are not worse (or better, damn it); this is simply to make sense later and to give you a glimpse into my experience. If you like this, use it; if not, don't.

Fire	That which we are passionate about. Vocations and attractions.
Water	That which we feel. Emotions, relationships—friendships, lovers.
Air	That which exists in the mind or is communicated. Thoughts, lessons, words.
Earth	That which we experience in a banal way. Jobs, money, family.

As always, these are distillations of my own distillations, but they represent what I frequently reach for.

Having described the elements to start, we should check our descriptions to make sure they're useful. As always, when I say useful, what I mean is that they're clear, sharp, and precise. That precision matters as a foundation, even if we're going to bend that foundation over time. The more our roots make sense now, both for the numbers and the elements, the more we're going to thank ourselves when we need to describe them to people who don't spend a big chunk of their day thinking about this.

And the more our clients[1] will thank us, because they'll understand what we mean more accurately.

Activity 3.2: Practicality

Objective: Ensure that elemental associates are specific and meaningful, rather than vague and impractical.

Why you should do this: Many clients are impressed by a reader's ability to see into their spiritual state or their general life experience. Then, in retrospect, they don't find the reading all that useful. This can be because of nebulous interpretations. Spending time making sure our meanings are useful and practical will create a more specific and clear interpretation in readings.

Instructions:
1. Review your elemental meanings, one at a time.
2. Explore whether your meaning has a practical relationship to life. Use these questions as a guide:
    a. If I used these words in casual conversation, would my friends know what I was talking about?
    b. If my boss explained a project using these words, would I know how to proceed?
    c. If I explained this to my boss in the context of a review or

---

1   I use "client" and "querent" interchangeably throughout this course. Neither feels quite right. "Client" seems to indicate that you "should" be charging for readings; "querent" is a made-up word I've never really loved. But, here they are, and in this case both mean "anyone you're reading for."

proposal, would my boss accept the explanation?

   d. If I tried to sell a product using these words to a skeptical buyer, would they walk away with a new gizmo?

   e. If someone used these words in a reading with me, would I feel like I could take specific action or have a clear picture of my situation based on them?

   f. Do I actually know what I mean by these words? Have I looked them up in the dictionary and validated my own definition of them?

3. If the answer to any of those questions is "no," reconsider your definition.

You may even look at my samples above and find that they've failed the activity I've put in front of you. And if you noticed that, well played. I am as guilty of vague meanings as anyone else. So, to make this easier on you, let's work though my own definitions and see how they can be improved. That may help you work through yours.

Fire	That which we are passionate about. Vocations and attractions.
Water	That which we feel. Emotions, relationships—friendships, lovers.
Air	That which exists in the mind or is communicated. Thoughts, lessons, words.
Earth	That which we experience in a banal way. Jobs, money, family.

Let's take each apart.

Fire: That which we are passionate about. Vocations and attractions.

How did I do? I think I get a solid C+ on this. Passion is something we can generally grab onto. And while most people don't think in terms of "vocation," we definitely think in terms of attractions. If I use the word "vocation," is it clear? Maybe. Many of us probably have to reach for a dictionary, unless we have a religious background. The word has an arcane, almost antiquated quality to it. When I think back to where I heard it, I realize that it came from my years in Catholic school. A vocation was what a nun or priest felt called to. In essence, it was one's higher calling. That fits "fire" to me—that which we are passionate about is frequently one's higher calling. But the word "vocation" itself may be unclear to the modern ear. "Attraction" is likely pretty clear, but anyone with a passing relationship to tarot might question what that has to do with the element. Attraction feels more like it equates with water, which most of us understand to do with relationships. When I wrote "attraction," what I meant was sexual attraction—the heat of romance. In essence, "lust." Thus, "attraction" is what I meant, but it's not super clear. How do I reconcile that? Well, I try again.

How's this:

Fire: What we are passionate about. Our higher calling, or what we view as our higher calling. What we desire or lust for, whether it's people or things.

That feels clearer to me, and in working through this I realize how I've been cheating myself for many years. I've never interpreted fire as having to do with a lust for things—but it makes total sense, especially in modern life. And maybe Pamela Colman Smith presupposed this, because if we think about that three of wands with the dude looking at the globe, one definitely could read a lust for stuff into that. I've also hedged my bets, or at least allowed for me to do that in a reading. We don't always know what our higher calling is, and what we lust to be our higher calling isn't always our actual calling. By adding "what we view as our higher calling" into the mix, I've allowed for the fact that there might be times when a gap exists between our actual higher calling and that which we desire as our calling. That said, my definition is now full of words that will be clear to most clients, and better yet it's revealed something new to me.

Let's try the next one.

Water: That which we feel. Emotions, relationships—friendships, lovers.
How did I do, here? I feel like this is a B or B+, objectively. All the words are clear and likely to make sense to anyone I'm reading for. I don't give it an A, though, because it's still vague. And this is a tough one, because let's be honest: emotions are nebulous, too. We don't always know what we're feeling, or how we feeling about our relationships. I have to be careful, because I could easily justify my existing definition that way. If I do that, I may be missing out on an opportunity to refine and clarify. So I persist. I also note that I put family in the earth box, but we certainly have feelings about family, and we definitely have relationships with them. I have to wrestle with this one a bit.

"That which we feel. Emotions, relationships—friendships, lovers." How can I improve that?

I'm going to start with first subject: feel. That's a word we throw around a lot, and as such we all think we know what it means. What is a feeling? I've defined it as emotions in my meaning, but is that it? I stub my toe and I feel pain. Is that a feeling? Is it an emotion? It's definitely a feeling, because I feel it, but it doesn't feel like an emotion. It feels like a reaction. I feel physical pain, but the emotions I experience will be anger or embarrassment, say. So when I say "water equals what we feel," am I right to limit that to only emotions? Can physical sensations be included, too? There's no reason not to, since physical sensation is as real as emotion. Is "sensation" a better word? It doesn't seem as clear as "feeling," but it does feel more specific. I want clear *and* specific, if I can possibly find it, though, because that's probably what I'll reach for in a reading.

What about this? *Water: What we feel, physically or emotionally. Sensations, emotions. What relationships cause, and what causes relationships.*

Better. But while I like the poetic quality of my last sentence, it's more poetic than it is practical. So, let's take that impulse further. What do I mean by, "What relationships cause, and what causes relationships"? I mean that relationships stir up emotions and sensations. I mean that sensations or emotions are frequently the impetus for forming relationships—or for *not* forming relationships. How can I clearly and specifically summarize that?

Let's try this. *Water: What we feel, physically and emotionally. Sensations, emotions. Relationships, and what causes them to form or not and continue or not.*

A little better. Notice that I changed "physically *or* emotionally" to "physically *and* emotionally." That link felt stronger, because, as we talked about with pain, it can be both physical and emotional. The clarification "sensations, emotions" may not be necessary, but it feels right, and since we're dealing with feelings in this element I'm going to go ahead and follow mine. The final sentence is less poetic, but it's definitely clearer.

This is maybe an A- now. I'm going to abandon perfectionism and move on.

I'll do Air and Earth, as well. If you feel ready, though, head back to the drawing board. Remember though that this isn't easy, and it's not meant to be. Reaching for clearer words isn't easy. If you had clearer words in mind, you probably would have used them the first time. But recognize that there was learning happening in the struggle to clarify and refine. Recognize, too, that you have resources available. In particular, the dictionary and thesaurus. Sometimes looking up a word and reading its definition is a great way to find a clearer way to say it. And sometimes the word itself is as clear as we're going to get. This activity can be like trying to define a color. What's blue? Define blue without using the word "blue" or any word that is a shade of blue—including "sky" and "bird." Not easy. But it's an interesting challenge and could be fun if we let it be. And so I say enjoy this process, annoying as it may feel, because it will pay off down the line. We're learning about something we love to do. Why not enjoy the game?

If you don't feel quite ready yet, here's Air and Earth. I'm not going to talk you through my mental process, but I will explain a bit about why I changed what I changed.

Original: Air—That which exists in the mind or is communicated. Thoughts, lessons, words.

Revised: Air—What we think and say. Our thought processes and our attempts to put those into words. Also, what we learn and how we learn it.

Commentary: Air is the most complex of the elements, because it encompasses a lot of ephemeral qualities. It's also a suit where I differ from many thinkers, because it is commonly viewed as a suit entirely or mostly of conflict. Certainly Waite-Smith painted that picture for us. But because I don't view any suit or number or card as entirely good or bad, I don't view air as conflict. It is the part of life that deals with the mind, as opposed to the heart (water) or the guts (fire). I give myself a B+ on this revision. But since I feel like my original was a D, I'm going to allow myself to be OK with this one for now. I have faith it will evolve over time.

Original: Earth—That which we experience in a banal way. Jobs, money, family.

Revised: Earth—Our daily duties, the things that impact our daily lives—the responsibilities of our jobs, our friends, and our families. The coming-and-going of money. Those things that keep our feet on the ground and our head out of the clouds.

Commentary: If Air is the most complex, Earth is the most important. This is the suit that addresses almost everything people want readings about. My original definition used the word "banal," which is both vague and kind of negative-sounding. The elements are neutral. The numbers and context give them light and shadow. Also, money makes sense, but jobs and family are addressed to a degree in Water (feelings, relationships) and Fire (calling). My aim here was to make it clear that what we're talking about is *job* versus *career*—what we do to make ends meet, which may or may not be our higher calling. Also, that how we feel about our families and friends is different from the responsibilities of living with them. Water is how we *feel* about them; Earth is our responsibilities to and with them. We love our kids. We long to protect and care for them. That's Water. We also have to feed them and clothe them and take them to soccer practice and pay for soccer practice and for the uniform and the ball. That's Earth. My definition comes a little closer to making that clear. The last sentence is really too poetic, but I feel like it is a good way of differentiating Earth from the other elements. Earth is made up of the other elements, so it's useful to remind ourselves of that and also that it is its own thing. I give myself an A-.

It's important that you know that I've gone through this process for real. I didn't have these final definitions and go back to more nebulous ones in an effort to make a point. The examples I gave initially are more or less the ones I've been working with about as far back as my learning about the elements. The revisions came through the process I described above.

I tell you that for two reasons: First, having written this course comes with the implication that I know more than you do about this. That's false. In the writing of this work, I'm learning. If I weren't, it would be oddly arrogant of me to assume anything I put in here would improve your process. I want you to recognize that as your guide, here, I'm also a learner. We're always learners. When we stop learning, I think, we run the risk of allowing ourselves to go stale. And staleness is bad. Especially when you're working on something like tarot. Second, our meanings and definitions can and should evolve over time. It's a good thing to revisit what we've been working with and explore how we could grow it. The definitions I gave you have worked for me for almost 20 years. I don't flatter myself when I say I've done good readings with those. I've also done bad readings with them, if that's worth pointing out. But I will do better readings now that I've spent time growing my experience of the elements.

Now: go do your homework!

Debrief: Vague elemental associations equal vague readings. Querents are sometimes impressed by what generalities we discover, but in retrospect they don't take much else away from the reading. Clarity and specificity are key.

Now, we move on to the next session. Before that, though, take a moment to explore how what you've learned will contribute to your tarot goals.

◊ Lesson 4: "Math" ◊

Don't panic. This will be fun and easy math. Or, if it's not easy, it should at least be fun. So far we've defined and refined the numerological meaning of numbers one through ten. We've also defined and refined the practical meaning of the suits/elements. Now it's time to bring them together.

I mentioned earlier that reading the pip cards is an equation. We started with *number + element = meaning.* The essential meaning of each of the pips is the combination of the element plus the number.

Now, though, it's time to expand it to *number + element + context + question = meaning.*

Let's explore:

In my world, the number one in *light* is potential and in *shadow* it is potential squandered. Fire is what we are passionate about. Our higher calling, or what we view as our higher calling. What we desire or lust for, whether it's people or things. My job as a reader is to bring that together and make it into meaning. To do the math.

To simplify, let's focus only on the *light* aspect of *one*, which is potential. I marry potential to the meaning of fire. So, the Ace of Wands: potential passion, potential higher calling, potential lust.

You may notice that I've yielded three divergent meanings. That's OK. Right now, we're worried just about this step, just about the equation of number + element = meaning. Remember that the real equation is number + element + context + question = meaning, but we're not there yet. And solving that equation is more fun and less stressful if we begin this way.

Let's try with the shadow aspect of one, wasted potential. I marry that to the meaning of fire. Thus: potentially wasted passion, wasted potential in one's higher calling, wasting potential on lust.

We don't have to overthink this. If you're doing this along with me, you may have come up with different interpretations. I hope you did. You should. That's why we need more than one tarot reader in the world. In that way, this differs from math. There isn't one right answer. But the analogy is useful: number + element = meaning. It's just that the answer is different for everyone.

Here's one more example.

Two (light): pairing, connection, balance + Air: what we think and say; our thought processes and our attempts to put those into words; also, what we learn and how we learn it = balanced thoughts or language, being of two minds, bipartisan communication, connecting to like-minded people.

 Two (shadow): discord, disconnection, imbalance + Air (see above) = difficulty focusing on one thing (disconnected thoughts), difficulty putting thoughts into words, partisanship, fighting with oneself.

 I'm pairing the number and the element and allowing them to speak to me, to tell me what they mean when they are partnered. I'm looking at the various keywords or concepts I've given each and playing with them to see if they make sense together. Not every keyword or concept for the number will make sense partnered with every keyword of concept of the element. The only thing to struggle with is if none of the keywords or concepts of the number seem to connect to any of the keywords or concepts of the element. If that happens to you, I recommend taking a break or revisiting your keywords to make sure they're really what you mean. But that happening is likely a 1 in 100 chance. Either way, you're about to find out.

Activity 4.1: Number + Element = Meaning

Objective: Partner each of the ten numbers of the pips with each of the four elements, to yield meanings for each combination.

Why you should do this: Because this is tarot reading, friends!

Instructions:
 1. Using the space below, sit with each number and element combo and devise a meaning from the combination.
 2. Take frequent breaks.

One + Air	
Two + Air	
Three + Air	
Four + Air	
Five + Air	
Six + Air	
Seven + Air	
Eight + Air	
Nine + Air	
Ten + Air	
One + Earth	
Two + Earth	

Three + Earth	
Four + Earth	
Five + Earth	
Six + Earth	
Seven + Earth	
Eight + Earth	
Nine + Earth	
Ten + Earth	
One + Fire	
Two + Fire	
Three + Fire	
Four + Fire	

Five + Fire	
Six + Fire	
Seven + Fire	
Eight + Fire	
Nine + Fire	
Ten + Fire	
One + Water	
Two + Water	
Three + Water	
Four + Water	
Five + Water	
Six + Water	

Seven + Water	
Eight + Water	
Nine + Water	
Ten + Water	

Debrief: This is tarot reading! You could take this and run with it as it is, but luckily you don't have to.

It should be made clear that the next activity is *not* to sit and memorize these. You will likely have internalized by now a relatively strong connection to the meanings of the numbers and the suits, but you shouldn't sit and commit all 40 of the combos to memory. As we've already learned, meaning is fluid and strongly affected by the other parts of the equation we haven't yet discussed. Having gone through this once, you will continue to go through this every time you sit down and do a reading in which pips appear. Shuffle, draw a card, find that it's the Three of Coins, figure out what three (growth) and coins/earth (duty, responsibility) mean to you (growing responsibility, growing family, growing income or growing bills). That's it!

But wait! I just drew the Three of Coins and came up with four different meanings! How am I going to figure out which of the four applies to this reading?

Funny you should ask.

But before I answer that, take a moment to record what you've learned and how it will help you come closer to your goals. And then, we're going to take a quick break. Don't worry, it'll be useful.

Interlude 2:
◊ On Questions ◊
and Ethics

When I began reading, the hot topic in tarot was ethics. I fully support ethical tarot reading. I fully support ethical behavior in all realms. One of the primary ethical concerns in the late '90s/early aughts, was rephrasing a question so that it didn't violate the reader's ethics. For example, a commonly held ethical practice is not to do third-party readings. An example of this might be that Douglas B. Witched arrives and asks us to do a reading exploring how Elaine B. Wildered feels about him. "Tell me if she loves me, if she's cheating on me, and what she's dreaming about at night!" Ethical readers believe that answering Doug's questions violates the privacy of the third party (Elaine), who doesn't know we're reading into her heart and mind. The ethical reader would advise Doug, "I can't see into Elaine's heart and mind, because that would violate her privacy. And anyway it's unlikely I could see what she's thinking or feeling, since she isn't the one who asked for the reading. I'm going to do a reading for you for the question, *what does Doug need to know about his relationship with Elaine?"*

It's a fair point, and a fair practice. I dutifully followed it for many years. Over time, though, I began to question myself. I had to rephrase 99.99% of the questions asked of me. I'd do a reading for Doug and answer the question I cooked up for him: "The Nine of Swords suggests you're thinking a lot about her, and that it's probably causing you some anxiety."

Uh, no shit! The fact that he asked you about her in the context that he did suggests that he is thinking a lot about her and experiencing some damn anxiety! Hey, Tommy B., way to tell him what he already knows!

Not only that, but way to also tell him, "Oh, by the way? What you asked was actually kind of stupid and immoral? So I'm basically going to save you from yourself."

Who am I as a reader to tell Doug what he wants or needs to know about anything? Especially if he didn't ask me to do that. There's an unintentional arrogance in the rephrasing of the question that, though nobody ever said anything to me, had to have at least poked at some questioners. But how to handle the dilemma of being asked to do things you couldn't do? Just tell people you couldn't read for them? What if 99.99% of the people you read for were asking questions you couldn't answer? Not read? And if you couldn't answer what people wanted to know, why even bother reading at all?

Add to those questions a general discomfort with the idea of predicting—remember my fear of death from the forward?—and I wound up in a crisis of belief that resulted in me not reading for others for a handful of years.

When I came out of that funk, I decided to go my own way—guiltily—and hope nobody noticed I wasn't being as ethical as I needed to be. Then in 2005, Teresa C Michelsen's *The Complete Tarot Reader: Everything you Need to Know from Start to Finish* arrived in my local bookstore. And I read this: "Rephrasing a question can come off as somewhat patronizing, and clients may perceive a lack of respect or understanding of their concerns. I do not believe that clients are incapable of asking the questions they really want to ask." Yes! This is what I was feeling! Someone had the guts to say it out loud!

Actually, I felt embarrassed—as though someone had caught me reading something I wasn't supposed to—but once that faded, I did feel all that "Yes!" stuff. Michelsen goes on to explore a handful of reasons why rephrasing is problematic, and what one may do instead. (It's a worthwhile read, and though it's currently out of print, it isn't difficult to find.) Since this chapter isn't *quite* about alternatives to that quandary, I won't quote her further. But reading that did give me the confidence to come out of the question closet. Of course I still hadn't solved the dilemma of what to do if someone asked me to peer into someone else's life, but I at least felt vindicated that I was right about the rephrasing issue.

Years later I would read Camelia Elias's frequent admonition: "Just read the damn cards." In Dr. Elias's world, you read the cards and answer the question you're asked, and you do it succinctly and honestly. You don't pull punches; you don't hem and haw. Granted, she's kind of a terse genius, and I'm kind of not. But I admire like hell her ability to cut through the dross and tell it like it is.

These days, I fall somewhere in between. I do believe there are things I shouldn't and can't read about (namely, those things that might get me sued). I say up front I won't read on health or legal issues. Legal, because of the litigious stuff. Health, because I honestly think if someone is coming to tarot instead of a doctor or healer for health advice, they're probably not in a place where they're going to believe good news or be able to internalize bad news in any productive way. Also because of my own constant fear of mortality (see Introduction). Beyond that, I try as much as possible to read on the question I'm asked.

In terms of third-party readings... Well, I don't know. I don't get asked them much, so it's not a question I have to wrestle with. But at my age and with my life experience, I'm not going to say I've never done them. And I'm not going to say I haven't been the person who asked me to do them. Other people affect us so much that understanding their intentions or motivations can be helpful. And that's not easy to do in life, especially because other people aren't always fully aware of their intentions or motivations. Is it an invasion of privacy? I don't know. Privacy in modern life is complex. So many thoughts and impulses are posted to social media. So much information is handed over to tech companies for the betterment of end-user experience. Is it really that much of an invasion of privacy if I as a tarot reader explore how someone else feels about you? I honestly don't know the answer to that question. What I do know is that tarot readings should be useful. Tarot readings should help us become active participants in our lives.

Lately, I trust my gut. I've been around the sun enough times to know when I feel good about something and when I don't. If a client's motive feels nefarious, I decline to read—regardless of the question. If the motivation feels right, if I see someone who needs objective information, I do what I can provide it. I always provide a disclaimer, and I always phrase my answer carefully. Because the other thing I've learned is that the key to ethical reading is in the phrasing of an answer.

Question: "I've got it bad for this girl in grad school with me. Does she love me back?"

Card drawn: Five of Swords, reversed.

My inner monologue: Conflict, disruption (reversed five) + What we think and say, thought process and attempts to put them into words, what we learn (air). Conflict isn't a good sign. What we think and say? She's thinking about conflict… Thoughts of him cause her conflict. If this were upright, she'd be thinking about shaking things up and that would be a good sign, but she's thinking about conflict and disruption. She views him as an intellectual disruption. Swords are also about attempting to put thoughts into words. She can't figure out how to express that to him. She's sure thinking about him a lot, but not in a good way.

What I might say if I were fearless: No. In fact, she doesn't know how to tell you she finds you grating and nowhere near her intellectual match. Move on, bro.

My actual response: When she thinks of you, it's in an intellectual way. Emotion doesn't look like it's playing a part here. This looks about as platonic as it could be.

It's the ethicist in me that stops me from giving the "fearless" answer. There's a part of me that feels like, were I trying to be really useful, I would be as blunt as that answer. But I also know that people build defense mechanisms to help them cope with the unpleasant vagaries of life. I recognize that when I've given people blunt feedback, most can't hear it. The words cannot be processed with the defenses they've built. So, I temper justice with mercy. I strain my thoughts through empathy, my own experience, and the recognition that I could be wrong about why she doesn't like him (even though I'm probably not). That's how I've decided to be useful—balance.

When people come to readers and ask questions on health or the feelings of others, generally one of two things is happening: Either they already know the answer and are hoping we'll give them reason to hope; or, they're afraid to get the answer they're dreading and so they ask someone who isn't an expert on anything other than reading cards. In the first case, it's more or less a last-ditch effort. In the second and often the first, they're protecting themselves by getting an answer they can dismiss if they don't like it. "It's only a tarot reader. What do they know?" They're still as in the dark as they always were, they're still as anxious about their state as they always were, but they can tell themselves they *tried* and it just didn't *work*, because who trusts a tarot reader, anyway?

Question: "I think my husband is cheating on me. Is my marriage over?"
Card drawn: Ten of Cups.

My inner monologue: Completion (ten) + Relationships (cups). Completed relationship? That's about as done as it gets.[1]

What I might say if I were fearless: Yeah, girl; it's over.

My actual response: Something that you felt good about seems to have reached the end. How do you think that might relate to your marriage?

In this case, I *want* to give the fearless answer. I give the other one because I want to put the onus back on the client. Is that the right thing to do? I feel like this person is more likely to accept it if she says the words out loud. You could easily argue that I'm opening the door to negotiation. The exchange could go a little something like this:

---

1   Note for those familiar with the Waite-Smith cards and its offspring: The Ten of Cups is among the most positive cards in the deck, with its happy family and rainbow. My interpretation is decidedly unhappy, at least at first glance. I've let ten (completion) + cups (relationships) equal the end of the marriage. That's far from the happy family depicted by Pixie Smith. This is one reason tarot fascinates me and why I'm happy to have both systems in my toolkit. If I had read for this client with a Waite-Smith deck, I probably would have gotten the Ten of Cups reversed, or something like the Eight of Cups (depicting someone walking away)—something that depicts leaving, or moving on. The Ten of Cups reversed in *this* system would have suggested to me that the marriage wasn't yet over, or the ending was being delayed, even if it was one the way out. The Eight of Cups would have suggested working really hard on the relationship. Completely different; totally fascinating. (It's also worth pointing out that this client has a partner who is clearly making her miserable. The Ten of Cups here, even though it says the marriage is over, is about as good a card as I could imagine—even if the client doesn't agree right now.)

ME: How do you think that might relate to your marriage?

CLIENT: The affair is over?

ME: Was that something you felt good about?

CLIENT: No, the idea makes me feel terrible.

ME: So, it's not that. What else could it be? Something you felt good about has reached the end of a cycle...?

CLIENT: ...I don't know. I can't think of anything...

ME: What have you felt good about, in relation to the question you asked?

CLIENT: I mean, I don't know...

ME: How did you feel about your marriage before you detected your husband's infidelity?

CLIENT: Oh, it was great.

ME: Yeah?

CLIENT: But I don't know what that has to do with the answer you gave me. I don't think you're very good at this.

ME: If you felt good about your marriage...? And something you felt good about has reached the end of a cycle...?

CLIENT: ...yeah...?

ME: ...what might that mean...?

CLIENT: *I don't know. That's what I'm paying you for!*

ME: *IT'S YOUR MARRIAGE! YOUR MARRIGE IS OVER! IT'S OVER, IT'S FINISHED, AND IT'S TIME TO MOVE ON! HE'S CHEATING ON YOU, FOR CHRISSAKES! HOW DID YOU NOT KNOW IT WAS OVER BEFORE YOU EVEN ASKED ME THAT QUESTION? YOU REALLY NEED A TAROT READER FOR THAT?*

CLIENT: (Pausing, then bursting into tears.) *Why are you so mean?* I'm giving you a bad review on Yelp!

Maybe someday I'll be brave enough to give the fearless answer. In the meantime, I continue to grow and experiment and to try to be as useful as I can.

This interlude on ethics, questions, and third-party readings may seem like a random digression, but it underscores the importance of questions. Much time in the tarot-reading world has been dedicated to the very question of questions. Imagine pulling the Ten of Cups or the Five of Swords reversed, used above, without a question.

Question: Give me a general reading.

Card drawn: Five of Swords, reversed.

My inner monologue: Uhhh… What?

What I might say if I were fearless: Yeah, I dunno.

My actual response: Time to shake up your thinking.

CLIENT: What's that mean?
ME: I dunno, man. You were the one who wanted a reading and didn't know what the hell you wanted to ask about. Maybe it means "shake up your thinking by not being so obtuse about getting readings!"

During my years struggling with the ethics of tarot, I resented people who asked me questions I felt like I couldn't answer. In my inimitable way, I now resent people who don't ask questions at all. Resent may be too strong. (Not much, but a little.) To me, the general reading is just that: general, generic, vague. General readings are, in my humble opinion, why many people who complain about readers not being very good had a bad experience. They didn't want to know about anything in particular, and they got a reading about nothing in particular. Then they complain that the reading wasn't about anything in particular!

These days I tell people that, in a more diplomatic way. "The more specific you are, the more specific I can be." And if I have someone in front of me who wants a general reading, I usually start with the unspoken question, "What area might this person want to devote some attention to?" I then give them a quick springboard and hope that a specific question arises. Not because it's easier for me to read (though it is), but because they will get more out of it and have an overall better experience (which they will).

There's an expression frequently used in corporate training: "If everything's important, nothing's important." I know it from Patrick Lencioni's business classic, *The Five Dysfunctions of a Team* (a book I recommend to anybody, *anybody*, who works with other people in *any* capacity), but I'm sure it existed before then. It means that if everything gets equal weight, nothing emerges as a focus. No progress gets made, because the things that deserve attention aren't getting it. Tarot readings are that way, too. Questions are the bounding box, the focus, the way we give attention to the things that need attention. As such, I'm overjoyed when people ask them—even if I have dubious feelings about their ethical underpinnings.

In that same vein, I've had times when I was asked a question and the card or cards that appeared didn't seem to relate. For example:

Question: What do I need to do to spice up my relationship?

Card drawn: Eight of Wands.

My inner monologue: The Eight of Wands?? No! This is a *cups* question—maybe pentacles. Wands are about art! About vocation! About what we need to be doing with our lives! The Eight of Wands has nothing to do with relationships! What do I do now? Maybe I'm not good at this. Maybe tarot doesn't work. I bet it doesn't. Why am I even *doing* this? I should just give up on—*wait!* I know! The wands card here means that the relationship isn't what they should be focusing on, right now. They should be focusing on getting their creative work out into the world![2]

At which point I would say: Hey, moron. I know you want to know about your relationship, but this card says that's not important. You should be focusing on your novel.

CLIENT: I'm not writing a novel.
ME: I don't know what to tell you. You clearly should be. This card says you should be submitting your novel.
CLIENT: I'm not a writer.
ME: This card says you are.

....

2   I'm using the Waite-Smith meaning, here, since this is based on real reading.

CLIENT: ...but my relationship...

ME: *What do you not get? Your relationship is meaningless! Your art! Your art! That's all that matters! Get that art out into the world!*

I look back on that way of thinking and I could smack me. First, I was projecting my own desires onto this client. Second, I was an idiot. Rather than wrestling with the question and the card in front of me, I let myself off the hook. I took the easy road. Instead of exploring what the Eight of Wands might suggest about the relationship, I decided the client was wrong and I had to correct him.

There may be times when the cards suggest that something is more important to a client than whatever they think is important. But there would need to be a lot of cards directing me there.

The cards drawn always answer the question asked, and if they don't seem to it's because of the reader, not the client, the question, or the cards.

Here's what should have happened:

Question: What do I need to do to spice up my relationship?

Card drawn: Eight of Wands.

My inner monologue: Look at all those big, stiff wands flying through the air!

Answer: Join the mile-high club, get a cabin at the top of the mountain and go to town on each other, have sex outside, have an orgy. Don't be passive, go out there and get it on.

The cards drawn always answer the question asked, and if they don't seem to, it's *my fault.* Not the client's. And certainly not the cards.

Lesson 5: Questions and Context

Questions and context are a complementary pair, so they are wed here. Questions provide context, but there are other kinds of context in a reading, too.

If you read the preceding interlude, you know that there's a lot to say on the topic of questions. "All" we need to worry about here is that the cards drawn *always* answer the question asked. That's our first context. The interpretation of the card depends on the question. The question is primary. All the work we did on elements and numbers earlier give us a foundation to answer the question, but, again, the question is primary.

That's important, because there are times when the meaning we know and the question asked can seem incongruous.

Question: How do I earn my boss's respect?
Card drawn: Six of Cups, reversed.

I'm a believer that all cards can answer all questions, but some are harder to parse than others. In my system, reversed sixes mean false harmony and vanity. Cups, for me, represent what we feel, physically and emotionally; sensations, emotions; relationships, and what causes them to form or not and continue or not. That gives us something that suggests feeling our boss is vain, or that we have false harmony.

The answer to earning my boss's respect is to feel she's vain or to have false harmony? Clearly not. This is where the context takes precedence. I have to answer that question with this card, and I somehow have to bend the meaning to the question. But that meaning doesn't make sense in response to this question! So maybe tarot doesn't work and I'm the worst!

Or, maybe we call back to Camelia Elia's assertion that meaning doesn't exist. Or, in my extrapolation of that: meaning is fluid.

And here's why I've been sharing my "inner monologues" in the reading samples I do throughout this book. So that you can see the path I take to land on my interpretation. In essence, it's like showing my work in math class.

So, to answer the question with the card, I need to do the math. Six of Cups reversed suggests vanity or false harmony. Clearly being vein or instilling false harmony isn't the way to earn anyone's respect. But wondering if my client *appears* vain or like she's more interested in false harmony than in addressing conflict could mean something. Perhaps this client's boss doesn't like people who appear vain or who don't engage in conflict because they're afraid of upsetting her. But does that mean my client is vain? I certainly don't want to suggest that to her. I don't really know her, and I don't want to upset her. But just because she isn't something doesn't mean that someone else can't perceive her that way. A common business cliché is that "perception equals reality." This card suggests that the boss may perceive my client as self-absorbed or resistant to engaging in genuine conversation with her. My client's boss might think that my client doesn't say anything personal because she doesn't think it's the boss's business or doesn't like the boss enough to share with her. Or that the client thinks opening up will somehow upset the false harmony they have between them. That's definitely possible. The cups suggest emotion, and that could be key. The reversed cup may suggest that my client isn't super comfortable with emotions in general. So, the boss wants to make a connection that the client hasn't been willing to engage in. The boss views the discomfort as vanity or something like it. What the client needs to do to earn her boss's respect is either express her discomfort about opening up with people or try to build a personal connection with her boss.

My interpretation: It looks like your boss may be misperceiving you, somehow. She may think that you're uncomfortable with her, and she's reading that discomfort in a negative way. You might be able to earn her respect by opening up to her. If you're actually uncomfortable, you might talk about how difficult you find opening up to new people; if you're not, you may want to try building a personal relationship with her as well as a professional one.

In this case, I've traveled far from my keywords of "vanity and false harmony." But the train of thought that brought me to my final destination took off from Vanity and False Harmony Station before arriving at Opening Up to Her Terminal.

This is really all reading is. It's a kind of word association with boundaries. The trouble is that we frequently start to doubt where the associations are taking us. But in *Tarot: The Open Reading*, Yoav Ben-Dov reminds us that nothing in a reading happens by accident. Following that train of thought is what's supposed to happen. The logical part of our brain, though, freaks out. "What are you doing?! The Six of Cups reversed means vanity and false harmony!" When the logical part of our brain starts to create doubt, it wants a moment to voice its anxiety. It's an opportunity not to doubt but to double check that we got on the right train. Are we asking ourselves the right questions? Have we followed a path that makes sense? It's a good opportunity to check in and check ourselves. But we can't let the quick check-in derail our thoughts. We can let it have its say. If we don't, it'll resent us and try to take over. But we can't let it take precedence. Most of the day, that part of our brain gets to do whatever it wants—from dictating our route to the office, to causing panic attacks out of thin air. When we're reading, it has to take a back seat to intuition (more on that later), and we have to exert our will over it, not the other way around.

With that, we arrive at our next activity.

Activity 5.1: Q&A

Objective: Using only the pip cards and the work we've done so far, answer questions with random draws of the deck.

Why you should do this: This is what we do every time we read the cards.

Instructions:

1. Using a pip-based or Marseille-style deck, remove one through ten of each suit, and place the rest of the deck aside.
2. Shuffle the pips.
3. Do five one-card readings for each of the questions in the table below.
    a. Following the example, try to keep your final answers concise.
    b. Achieving concise answers generally takes some effort, so you use the middle column to "show your work." Use that space to help you draw a line between the card's association and your final answer.

Example: What is the real cause of my work-related anxiety?

Card Drawn	"Math"	Final Answer
Ten of Coins	Ten = completion; coins = duty, responsibility. Completion of responsibility. That sounds good, like the end of a project. But what if the client is worried that once he's finished his work on whatever he's doing now, it's going to be the end of his employment—or that he won't have anything to offer after that because he'll have used up all his energy on this project?	Your anxiety stems from the idea that your work may come to an end either because the project comes to a close or because the money that funds your work runs out.

	So the anxiety stems from responsibilities coming to completion… That's the main thing. Coins also equal money, so there could be anxiety around funding for his program ending.	
Four of Cups, reversed	Four reversed = conservatism, rigidity; cups = What we feel, physically or emotionally. This suggests feeling conservative or rigid, so things are fluid in this environment, but the client doesn't thrive well in that, and it's making him anxious. It could be politically; maybe there are a lot of people talking about progressive politics, and it's causing him to feel like his more conservative views are out of place. It's hard to say with one card, and I don't want to say much about this person's views, yet, since it's hard to tell. So I'm probably better off focusing on the "fish out of water" idea.	The environment around you feels like it's ever changing and fluid, but that's not how you like to work and the lack of structure is making you edgy.
Ace of Wands	One = seed, potential; wands = What we are passionate about. Our higher calling, what we desire or lust for. This one seems pretty clear. The conflict between a "day	The anxiety stems from the gap between where you feel you should be and where you are. Whether you want to advance in your company or be part of

	job" and the potential we feel for finding our higher calling. But am I just going to the obvious place too easily? What else could this suggest? That the client isn't growing fast enough? Aces are seeds, so that could be it—but I'd be more inclined to go with slow growth if the card were reversed. Upright, it suggests potential and growth are definitely in process, so if anything, it's the client who isn't proceeding fast enough. I don't know, though, because she hasn't told me. Either way there's a disconnect between the need to be part of one's higher calling and one's current state. So regardless of the reason why, there is conflict between one's current position and what one views as one's true place.	some other venture, it's the fact that you're not fully where you want to be that makes you edgy.

I only did three for example, but I recommend doing all five if you can. If you want to do one for each of the questions, then go back and do a second for all, then a third, that's fine, too. I don't think you lose either way. What you gain by doing this, though, is exploring how the pips work in connection to questions, and how different cards can answer the same question.

I recommend writing down your work so that you can visit it later. When I scroll through my Instagram, I see readings that I did and sometimes wonder what the path was that got me there. If I wanted to, I could probably work backwards—but it's unlikely I'll make the same connections. The readings are products of their time, and of the state of my mind when I did them. If I were to ask the same question and draw the same cards today, I would likely come up with a different answer. How different is tough to say, but the version of me that read the cards two months ago is gone, and the version of me who is here reading them today will have a different view. Being able to see how you arrived at an interpretation can be helpful.

And now it's your turn.

1. What does he think of me?
Card drawn:
Math:

Final answer:

2. I'm looking for work. What's the best place to focus my energy?

Card drawn:

Math:

Final Answer:

3. I'm really in love, but I can't figure out if I should confess my feelings. What happens if I do?

Card drawn:

Math:

Final answer:

4. Where are my lost keys?
Card drawn:
Math:

Final answer:

5. How much does my boss know about what I did?
Card drawn:
Math:

Final answer:

Debrief: This is what we do every time we read the cards.

I've thrown some curveballs, here. That was intentional. I'm not sure if someone came to me and asked me where their lost keys were I'd actually be able to give them a clue. But if you wrestled with that one, then kudos! Likewise, the question about the affair. The reason I chose what I chose is to prove that if we wrestle hard enough, we can usually come up with an answer. If I were faced with the keys question, and I randomly pulled the Seven of Swords, I'd probably just go ahead and throw in the towel. Seven = introspection; swords equal what we think and say. What could that possibly mean? But sitting here and wrestling with that I immediately think, "they're at your therapist's office!" – the place where you go to be introspective and think and say things. That could be the confessional at church, the therapist, or the bar where you just unloaded your mind to the sympathetic bartender. Something like that, but the place where you go to talk about your inner state is where your keys are hiding.

One thing that frustrates tarot readers, and makes many a novice quit altogether, is that many of us give up on readings too easily—especially when reading for ourselves. We draw three cards to answer a question, we look at them, we realize suddenly they have no connection to what we asked, and we give up. We don't wrestle with them enough, don't talk through the connection, and so we decide that reading for ourselves is too hard. It *is* hard; harder than reading for others, because we do lack objectivity. But more than objectivity, what we frequently lack is tenacity.

A month or so ago, I was stuck with a problem at work: how to teach adults geography in the course of seven thirty-minute sessions. I'd tried three different outlines and threw each one away as useless. Finally, I elected to do an advice reading for myself. I shuffled and drew the Three of Wands, the Five of Swords reversed, and The Magician reversed. I looked at that hot mess, and I came very close to sweeping the cards back into the deck and repeating the myth that reading for oneself is fruitless. Instead, I sat down and I did the math for each of the cards, and then

I crammed those associations together and came up with a plan that wound up solving the problem. The three was about growing passion, the five reversed was about giving the middle finger to traditional ways of thinking, and the magician reversed was about deception. I wrestled with that, and I realized that the key was to start by igniting the passion—interest—of the adult learners, to shake up the way we'd always done it, and to deceive them into learning. That allowed me to come up with a plan that sparked the interest, revitalized the learning process, and tricked everyone into learning something new. If I hadn't forced myself to wrestle with those cards, I wouldn't have gotten that idea.

The real key to reading for ourselves is tenacity.

That three-card reading is a nice segue into our next topic, which is context.

As I already shared, the question itself is one kind of context. It provides a bounding box or a limit to the potential meaning of the cards. Whether the card is reversed or not provides another kind of context, if you use reversals.

The third kind of context is the other cards in the spread, and that's the kind of context we're going to focus on now.

The interplay of the cards is as important as the interplay of the cards and the question. If we think about the examples I gave above, for the question about work anxiety, each of those answers would have been different if I'd done a three-card spread. Even if one of the cards was the one I drew, the interplay would have shaded the meaning.

Let's look more closely. The question was, "what is really the cause of my work-related anxiety?" The first card drawn was the Ten of Coins.

I decided that meant that the anxiety was caused by the feeling that the project he was working on would be over and there would be nothing left for him to do, or that the money funding his project would run out.

Let's say that the Ten of Coins was the middle of a three-card spread, flanked by the other two cards I drew: the Four of Cups reversed and the Ace of Wands. I could, theoretically, just give the same three answers I gave above. But thanks to Robert M. Place's work in *Tarot: History, Symbolism, and Divination,* I've come to see that the cards in a three-card spread are one answer. In a way, they are one card. The aim is to mush them together into a single answer, instead of giving three different answers to the same question.

So now the equation looks something more like this:

[Four reversed + cups] + [ten + coins] + [one + wands] = meaning

Or

[Feeling emotionally rigid or conservative] + [responsibilities or funding ending] + [potential for higher calling] = meaning

More complicated math, but the process is still the same. I have to solve for the meaning with the cards I've got, and I need somehow to make them make sense together.

There are a few ways to go about this, and none of them are wrong. They will likely yield the same answer. One way is the linear way: add the first two together to get a meaning, then add that meaning to the third:

([Feeling emotionally rigid or conservative] + [responsibilities or funding ending]) + [potential for higher calling] = meaning

The other way is to start with the card that "feels" most active in the spread. In that case, I go from math to grammar. Which card in the reading feels most like a verb, or an action? Whichever it is, I start there and look at the relationship between the other cards. In this case, the most active one to me feels like the Ace of Wands. It's the last card in the spread, so I might read backward:

([Potential for higher calling] + [responsibilities or funding ending]) + [feeling emotionally rigid or conservative] = meaning

Whatever way you decide to plan your attack, the key is tenacity.

Let's work our way through it. For the sake of simplicity, I'll use the linear method (the first one above). As always, I'll write out my inner monologue for you so you can see how I arrived at my final destination.

The combination of coming to close on a project (Ten of Coins) and being naturally uptight (Four of Cups, reversed) is strange. It's possible that this person's rigidity may actually be causing the project to come to a close. If they've been inflexible and made their feelings known, the people who hold the purse strings may be saying that it's not worth the money to continue. It's possible that the opposite is true, the funding coming to a close is amping up the person's rigidity—but since I'm looking at this in a linear row, the first card wants to be the focus, the subject. I'm more drawn to thinking that the rigidity might be the central cause. It's difficult to know for sure, because this person isn't sitting right in front of me, but luckily I have a third card in the spread. The Ace of Wands, representing potential for higher calling. Looking at these cards as a set, it's hard for me not to feel that my initial impulse is reinforced—the emotional rigidity is causing the project to come to a close. In fact, this person seems to have a sense that they are meant for greater things, and their passion lies there. I don't have any swords cards to explore how this person communicates (though I could draw one), but I know that the combination of water (cups) and fire (wands) make steam. Steam gushes and erupts; it is hot and can build up in closed environments, creating a pressure cooker. That makes me wonder if this person has a temperament that isn't suited to the more practical (coins) environs of their workplace. These temperamental cards appear on both sides of the coins card, so in essence they're surrounding it, even trapping it.

Now I've got a picture of a temperamental person who is rigid and who feels that he's got better things to do, and a project that is nearing completion—potentially because of his attitude.

That's an interesting portrait, and it's tempting to share it. But that's not the answer to the question I was asked. The question was, "what is the really the cause of my work-related anxiety?" So now I have to figure out how that relates to the question, and I have to try to phrase it in a way that won't offend the client so much that he stops listening to me.

What could this mean? Here's my final answer: Your anxiety is stemming from the fact that you've been openly unhappy doing this work. Now that this project is coming to a close, you feel like you may not be asked to stay on.

What happened to the stuff about the emotional rigidity and the feeling like he has better things to do? Frankly, to the client, it's not that important. He doesn't want to know what the individual cards mean, he wants to know the answer to his question. The meaning of those cards helped me suss out the answer, but I don't need to talk about each individual card unless he asks me to. If he looks at me after I give my response and says "prove it," I can talk about how I arrived at that decision. But my job isn't to teach him how to read tarot. It's my job to answer the question he asked.

Also, if I go into detail about the specifics of what I saw, I need to be careful about accusing him. My impression throughout the math of that reading was fairly negative. That isn't interpretation; that's bias. I don't know the circumstances behind how unhappy he's been. Just because it feels to me based on these cards like he has a higher calling doesn't mean I have the right to judge it. I saw somebody in my mind's eye who was pretentious and thought he was better than the work he was doing. Bias. What if he happened to work in a religious organization that he thought should be focusing on the feeding and housing of the poor and had instead been spending a huge amount of money funding a campaign to deny gay people the right to marry? He felt that his church should be focusing on helping the poor, and he has been vocal about it. He got into the church because he was passionate about his mission but discovered that the politics of the work weren't in line with what he believed. That's someone I'm more sympathetic to, but if I go into with my initial impression, then I've said to him: "You've alienated the people you work for because you think you're better than they are, and you think you know better than they do, and they're not going to extend your contract as a result. Way to be a jerk." No. It's better, as much as possible, to keep answers neutral. Even if we fancy ourselves tell-it-like-it-is readers who give the fearless answers I wrote about in the interlude, we don't get to be judge and jury.

Activity 5.2: Context

Objective: Explore how adding cards to the spread affects the meanings of each card.

Why you should do this: This is real-life practice.

Instructions:
1. Using the same questions as the prior activity, perform the same series of readings using three cards to answer each.
    a. *Optional: Start with the cards you drew in the previous activity, and then add two more to it. Explore how its meaning evolves as other cards join it in the spread.*
2. Show your work.
3. Take breaks.

Questions:
What does he really think of me?

1. I'm looking for work. What's the best place to focus my energy?

Cards drawn:

Math:

Final answer:

2. I'm really in love, but I can't figure out if I should confess my feelings. What happens if I do?

Cards drawn:

Math:

Final answer:

3. Where are my lost keys?

Cards drawn:

Math:

Final answer:

4. How much does my boss know about what I did?

Cards drawn:

Math:

Final answer:

5. If I continue with this affair, will it really hurt anyone?

Cards drawn:

Math:

Final answer:

Debrief: Using the same questions allows us to continue on the path we started last time. In reality, the questions we're asked as tarot readers don't vary as much as the combinations of cards that answer them. Using the same questions, even taking the optional path of starting with the same card, helps us see more clearly the overall theme of this lesson. Namely, that context changes meaning: the question we're asked, the cards that are drawn, the combination of those cards, and even our mood at the time of the interpretation.

How important is our mood? Sometimes not at all, sometimes very. There are days when question six, above, may not strike us. There are other days in which we found out dear friends are splitting up because of an infidelity, and our sensitivity to the issue of who gets hurt in affairs could have swords looking like daggers and wands looking like clubs.

Nothing in a reading is an accident, as Yoav Ben-Dov says. Our mood is part of that equation and will shade the meaning of the cards in front of us. It's worth knowing that and noting it as we sit down to read. It's also worth considering whether we're in the right frame of mind to answer a question. If I'm stinging from having been cheated on, will I truly be able to answer the question in front of me? It's a tough call. If nothing else, knowing that it will factor in can be helpful.

Choosing three-card readings for this practice activity wasn't accidental, either. I already gave a tip of the hat to Robert M. Place's *Tarot: History, Symbolism, and Divination.* It's about as brilliant a book on tarot as has ever been published. While its ultimate focus is the Waite-Smith deck, he goes into the history of tarot—of cards in general—and includes the pre-Gold Dawn decks, in a way most books that I'd encountered to that point had not.

Part of the system he explores in this book is the idea of using three cards for each position in a spread. So that if you were doing a three-card reading, you would in fact do a nine-card spread, each set of three representing one meaning. He reasons this not only provides more information, but exponentially increases the potential combinations possible in a reading.

I didn't require much convincing. I rarely use fewer than three cards in a reading and am a devotee of the nine-card spread: three rows of three. The technique of reading this spread comes more from cartomancy in general, than tarot specifically. My love affair with the nine-card stems from its flexibility, its fluidity, and the sheer amount of information one receives from it.

There are countless variations on how people read it. In the example, here, we'll look at the simplest: read each of the three rows for meaning, then read each of the three columns.

It's worth noting that a spread answers the question asked, and, as such, it's important that we not get sidetracked. We're reading all three rows and all three columns to answer the question, which means we have to keep that in mind as we go along. It is tempting to look at the spread as exploring different issues—and it may seem to. It doesn't. All the combinations we're exploring are shedding more light on the question (unless it's a general reading—but even in that case, I feel readings are most effective when they direct our attention toward one issue).

Let's work through an example together, before we practice on our own.

To mix things up, let's start with a different question than the one I used earlier. We will continue using only pips for the moment.

Question: How much relationship potential is there for me and Emil?

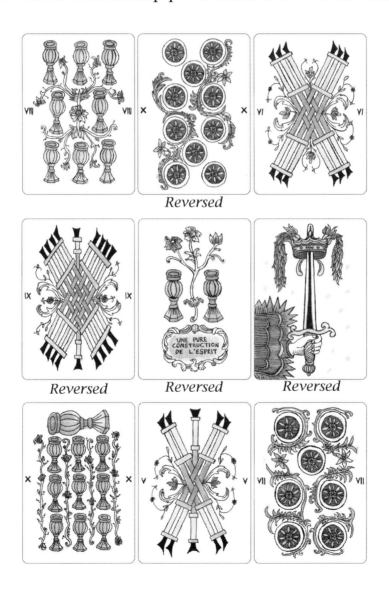

Inner monologue: I'm going to start with the bottom row to see what the foundation is, what everything else is sitting on. That seems like a good place to start, because if the foundation for the relationships isn't solid, that'll be an interesting sign.

None of the cards in this row are reversed, so there's a stability there, but I have a five smack-dab in the middle. Disruption. In this case, disrupted passions, maybe lustiness. This is upright, so I'm looking at this in its "light" mode, its productive or active mode, so that could actually be a good thing—this relationship is a good mix up for her, sexually. The Ten of Cups suggests completed feelings, and the Seven of Coins means looking inward to explore one's duties. I'm going to take "completed feelings" to mean "complete" as in "whole," rather than the sense of "finished." The Seven of Coins suggests that there may be some conflict between passion and responsibility. But it's upright, so we're also looking at this card in its productive way. So, there's a deep inner commitment to duty. In a relationship that's not a bad thing. And having some grounding energy is useful, especially given the fire and water energy creating some heavy steam. So the foundation this relationship sits on, at least for her, is a devotion to her responsibility to self that also satisfies her sexually and makes her feel emotionally whole. Not a bad start.

The top row starts with the Eight of Cups, also not a bad start—doing the emotional heavy lifting is something people don't always commit to. The reversed Ten of Coins is an interesting counterpoint, though, to the seven in the bottom row. The reversed ten suggests lingering responsibility that isn't being focused on—so there's a conundrum of being willing to do the emotional labor, but not finishing the life stuff that also needs attention. The Six of Wands tells me that this relationship feels damn good. There's that passion again, and it is beautiful. (Note that wands in this reading have nothing to do with work or creativity, which I frequently associate with passions—higher calling. In this reading, wands are all about heat.) This row suggests that the emotional labor feels way sexier than the life stuff that requires her attention.

The middle row is all reversed, which out of the gate suggests "head over heels," doesn't it? And that well may be, but for the reversed Two of Cups in the center smack-dab in the middle of the reading. That's giving me a vibe of disconnection, sort of an emotional disparateness.[1] Not good. But, I have two other cards to flavor this one with. Nine of Wands rev. suggests uncertainty, even perfectionism. Interesting, for this reading. So far, all the wands have had a relatively positive bent, here, but this suggests some anxiety about this passion. It makes me feel like she worries she won't be able to bring the passion to fruition—as though it'll burn out and become unsustainable. The Ace of Swords is stunted potential, in terms of intellect or communication. Does she feel like they don't actually have that much to talk about? It's not uncommon for folks who have deeply passionate connections to suddenly discover that when the passion wears off, they don't have much to say to each other. I have to tie all of this into the question she's asked, and that's going to help me limit my options. I'm going to follow my instinct, because it connects to the question: The potential is somewhat limited because emotional growth

---

1   In fact, when I read this way, I use a trick learned from Kelly Fitzgerald, of The *Truth in Story*. I lay the middle card down first and pair it with the card in the upper left. If I were doing that in this reading, I'd be pairing the Two of Cups rev. and the Eight of Cups—which would tell me that this relationship isn't growing because it's too much work.

and passionate connection are somewhat unsustainable, because they don't have much to talk about beyond that.

So far, it looks like there's a fair amount of potential for the relationship—*if* they have anything in common beyond sex.

Let's look at the columns:

Eight of Cups; Nine of Wands, rev.; Ten of Cups: Emotional work, passionate insecurity, emotional completion. Summary: the intensity of this emotional connection makes her freaked that she may not be able to hold on to this passion for long.

Ten of Cups, rev.; Two of Cups, rev.; Five of Wands: This comes out of nowhere, but I'm wondering if there are past relationships that haven't been resolved that are shaking up her sense of security in this relationship. I think that because of the reversed ten (incomplete) and two (pairing). Maybe the middle row suggests what it does because she has leftover junk from other relationships? Because so much of what was in the reading to that point was relatively positive.

Six of Wands; Ace of Swords, rev.; Seven of Coins: The trickiest combo, so far. And I frequently find that this third column is frequently a head scratcher. This is the only combo that doesn't have a cup in it, so it makes me think that it has nothing to do with relationship. *But:* I'm answering a relationship question, so whatever I interpret has to contribute to the relationship question. I've got beautiful passion, stunted intellectual potential, and dutiful introspection. What's this mean? She's really considering the practicality (Seven of Coins) of this relationship: can really profound passion carry a relationship if they're not connected, intellectually?

If I wanted to, I could also read the X—diagonally from top left to bottom right, and top right to bottom left. Sometimes that's helpful, especially if you've gotten a mixed message. In this case, I've already got so much information that anything else would just muddy the water. There's such a thing as information overload, and in this case that would contribute. I feel a commitment to read all the cards, because that will add nuance. But there comes a point where one has to begin doing the real work.

Commentary: It's tempting to end the reading here, because if I've spoken all of this out loud, it's likely about twenty minutes worth of explanation. That's a lot. But I haven't answered the question, fully. It may feel like I have—six times. But I haven't. I've laid the groundwork for the answer, but I haven't answered the question. And that's something that we sometimes forget. We've interpreted six three-card spreads. Those six three-card spreads are the research. The thesis needs to be formed.

From what I can see, the relationship has potential—but there is a degree to which the physical and emotional outweigh the intellectual. She's worried she won't be able to sustain the passion and emotional connection, because that's something she's struggled with in the past. In fact, there may have been another relationship that she hasn't fully resolved that was similar.

Final answer: The relationship does have potential. It's certainly passionate and emotionally satisfying. There are some questions about sustainability, though, so it's worth asking what you have in common beyond the physical and emotional. What do you have to talk about besides romance? Also, there may be some unresolved habits from previous relationships that could pop up, here, so take a look at those. Any past issues likely center on the issues of sustainability and having more than just romance in common.

Commentary: I feel generally confident in my answer, and I based it on what the reading told me. Looking at the answer I do have a sense that this could be said about a lot of relationships. My own experience has taught me that early on, relationships are full of fire and water—love and passion. Because those are the two volatile elements of tarot (air and earth tend to be more sustainable, because they're less likely to create steam), they can burn out. Water can put out fire; fire can evaporate water. Many relationships start off hot and heavy and peter out after a while, especially when partners discover they have nothing else in common.

There is a temptation to doubt the answer. "Surely there's something more profound to say, something more original." Resist that voice. The job of a reading isn't to be profound; it's to answer the question that was asked. The client didn't say, "tell me something about this relationship that'll blow my mind!" She asked if there was potential. We answered that question, using evidence from the cards. Maybe the client hopes for a mind-blowing answer, or maybe we want to impress the client. Doesn't matter. The question was the context, and we have to stay in that bounding box. If the client asked me to tell her something mind-blowing, I would have approached each set of three with a completely different context and likely would have wound up with a different interpretation. Or maybe I wouldn't have. Maybe the most mind-blowing thing about this relationship is that it runs the risk of combusting if there isn't more connection between them. I don't know, because I didn't read for that. And as you can see, doing a reading on that question would take a while.

Throughout the math of the reading, we should check in with the question to make sure we're on the right path. If we start to veer too far off, we can realign. It's simply a matter of asking ourselves, "How does that interpretation connect to the question?" Then continuing the association. That's all. But if we don't do it, we might end up at a destination that we didn't intend. The question is our GPS. If we keep referring to it, we will arrive where we need to—even if we take some wrong turns along the way.

Activity 5.3: Nine-Card Readings

Objective: Use skills developed so far to perform nine-card readings.

Why you should do this: At the risk of being repetitive, this is reading!

Instructions: I'm going to ask you to work with the same questions you've worked with throughout this lesson. I changed my example, above, to keep your interest, but I feel that it's important to explore how the connection between the question and the cards chosen changes the reading. Further, if you come back to these readings at any point in the future (and you should do that), having the progression of the questions will interest you more than a series of random questions. That said, because nine-card readings require more time, you don't need to do all six. Choose two or three that you would like to engage with.

1. Choose three questions from the examples used in this chapter.
2. For each question, perform a nine-card reading. Take into account what we've talked about, and show your work.
3. Perform two additional nine-card readings for each of your three chosen questions, and again show your work.
4. Throughout, be sure to check yourself against the question. How is your interpretation answering what was asked? If it's not, make sure you realign yourself. Use the question as a guide or compass to keep you on the right track.
5. Make sure you take breaks after each.

Debrief: By this point, you've gotten a fair amount of practice working with context and questions. We haven't really explored general readings all that much, and that's primarily because the concern so far has been specificity. You can use these techniques for general readings, but it's worth coming up with a method that will help you narrow the scope a little bit. You may, for example, use the left-hand column to give you a theme for the reading, or use the bottom row for foundation. In the sample I used above, I could say that the Eight of Cups, Nine of Wands reversed, and Ten of Cups tells me that there is a relationship that's been working and it's nearing its completion, because the passion has been losing steam. (That's a quick example). If that client verifies that's so, you can base the reading on that theme. Then you've turned a general reading into a more specific one and given yourself some context.

I harp on context because when people find themselves discouraged with a tarot reading, it is frequently because they didn't hear anything they didn't already know. Readings have a way of doing that, but people want *REVELATIONS!* They're more likely to get those if they actually ask a question.

Still, it's not within the scope of our reading life to tell people what they want. If they want a general reading, they're entitled to one. I prefer to make it clear that the more they tell me, the more I can read into the cards. But it's ultimately up to them.

People are complicated creatures. They have wills of their own and they want what they want. We can't force them to want something else. It's our job in part to respect that.

Which brings us to an elegant transition: out of the pips and into the court. But before we get there, as always, take the opportunity to journal about how what you've learned that will take you closer to your goals.

◊ Lesson 6: The Courts ◊

I'm just going to say it: The tarot court drives me insane. In nearly 20 years of reading, my relationship with court cards has evolved and grown to a mutual if grudging understanding of one another. That said, I am not among those who favor revising them out of the tarot or making them into something else. More on that shortly.

In the meantime, if you already have experience with tarot and you're happy with your method of reading the courts, you could skip these lessons. The thing that makes Marseille or pip-style decks so different from Waite-Smith decks are the pips and, to a degree, the trumps. If you're happy with your courts, keep them.

On the other hand, part of the goal of this book is to deepen your tarot practice, and ground it in some practical techniques. So, with that in mind, I encourage you to keep reading and potentially find new things in those sixteen temperamental cards.

For all their annoying tendencies, I think the court belongs in the deck. I'm not wild about decks that revise the court into elemental combinations (fire of fire, water of fire, air of fire, etc.). While those elemental associations can be helpful, the reason that the court still holds currency in tarot is because they are the people. They're the "us" of the deck. And tarot is about us. They are the humans in our lives. That's important in all systems of reading tarot, but especially in Marseille and similar decks, because we don't see as many people as we do when reading a Smith-inspired minor arcana. Though the Page, Knight, Queen, and King may be born of a royalist and patriarchal history, though they cause readers of all stripes headaches when they show up in spreads, the bottom line is that they need to be there, because there are people in our lives and those people have an impact on us. Whatever we call them, there should be people in the deck, not just elements, and they should have people-like attributes. We can't avoid it, and we can't avoid them.

Sometimes the court represents the tall, dark strangers in our lives; sometimes they represent us, i.e., the querent. Because why shouldn't this be as complicated as possible? As well suited as the tarot might be to reading, it wasn't designed for that, and nowhere is that clearer than the court: a group of cards that is sometimes us at different parts of our journey, and sometimes the people around us. And there is never a sure way of knowing who or when or what. Even the Kabbalah seems to fit tarot perfectly—except for the courts.[1]

---

1   We won't touch on Kabbalah, by the way, but it's worth noting how elegantly it

One of the first steps in reconciling the courts in our readings is deciding how we're going to work with them.

Let's start by pausing to consider how tarot works. (Am I stalling? Maybe, but hang in there.) I don't know what makes the world the kind of place where a deck of cards can help us explore our lives, but I know that it can do that. One of the reasons it can, I think, is because we give it rules. We say, for example, that wands equal our passions and our higher calling. We assign a general meaning to each part of the tarot, and while we allow for fluidity in reading, we don't suddenly decide, "Oh, wands actually represent housing!" No, once we decide that wands equal fire, we stick to it, more or less, throughout our reading lives. We obviously grow and change, and so does our understanding of what that suit relates to, but before we sit down to do a reading, we don't suddenly decide cups actually represent food. We make a decision about what cups or wands or The Fool means, then we shuffle the cards and we draw.

What I'm getting to is that we set up rules for ourselves and for the cards. We know going in what cards represent what, and so when we shuffle and draw, the context for that isn't just the question and the relationship of the cards to each other, but also to the meaning that we've given them. What I mean is that if we decided that cups mean food, the act of shuffling and drawing the cards would involve that consideration, and the cards I need to see would show up. We tell the cards what they mean, and in the shuffling and drawing, the cards we need to see appear.

Clear as mud? It seemed so much clearer before I sat down to type it.

matches minus the sixteen royals. Attempts to make them connect to the four emanations seem clumsy to me, but they've worked for many folks.

But the idea is that we tell the tarot the rules, and it follows them. The cards and our minds have an agreement. "I think these cards mean this." The deck says, "OK. So, when you shuffle and draw me, I'll make sure to order myself accordingly."

Why this explanation? Because the court cards follow similar rules. Those cards get frustrating in readings not because the cards themselves are inherently vague, but because we've made vague agreements with them. We essentially say to them, "OK, you kinda mean this, but also that, and sometimes this, and we'll just wing it when we need to." And the cards are all, "you got it boss." And then they behave like ill-mannered teenagers, because we haven't given them boundaries.

If we want the courts to have make sense, then we have to give them that sense. We have to tell them the rules, and they will follow them. That's "all" there is to it. I say "all" because, of course, that means making some decisions. And that's a pain in the neck. Really, anything is possible, and that's not good—because if anything is possible, then where do we start?

At the very beginning: The court cards are people.

OK. Now. We have to make some more decisions. Are the court cards *always* other people? Or, are they always aspects of ourselves?

I need to have both. I don't want to give that up. So, no, in my case, they're not always other people. Sometimes they're aspects of us.

That complicates things, though, because I now have a vague rule. If I really want to make this easy on myself, I would just decide here and now that the courts are one or the other, so that I don't have to guess. But I've spent years thinking about them as both, and I find it valuable to have both options in my pocket. That means I need to set up another rule, or series of rules, that help me figure out when the courts are the client and when they're people in the client's life.

Making those choices gives me anxiety. But if I want my readings to be clearer, I need to make those choices. I could use my intuition, and will, but I've been doing that for years, and it hasn't made the reading any less frustrating. We know the definition of insanity is doing the same thing over and over and expecting a different result. If I want clarity, I need to make up my mind. I can change it later, but I need to make it up now.

One rule I can use is the question. If the question is about the client *in particular*, about her own journey or path, I can decide that in such cases the court card represents an aspect of her personality that will play a big part in her development. Questions where I might take this track include:

1. How do I advance toward my higher calling?
2. How do I make peace with my feelings about this?
3. What is going to make me happiest right now?
4. What do I need in my life to feel whole?

These are questions that focus on the client's inner emotional or psychological journey in life, and while other people will, of course, affect it, the reins are largely in the hands of the client. As such, I could allow all the court cards to represent her.

Then, when the question clearly involves other people, I could let those court cards represent others.

Not incredibly tidy, but neater than the free-for-all I have used in the past.

Another method is right out of Waite's book—literally. Have the client look through the courts and choose a significator, or choose one for them. Rather than placing it down on the table, mix it into the shuffle, and if it shows up in the reading, you know what card is the client. This would be similar to the man and woman cards in Lenormand.

You could say that all pages and queens, regardless of age/race/gender, are the querents, and all knights and kings are those in their lives—or any combination thereof. You could do the same with suits. The courts in the suit of cups and coins represents the querents, the other suits are others in their life. None of that feels particularly elegant, though, does it? And we're going from a free-for-all, where the courts could mean anything, to severely limiting who and what they could explore.

A tempting option is to use reversals. If the court card is upright, it represents someone else; if the card is reversed, it goes internal and represents the client's state. If you don't use reversals generally, this could be the solution we've all been looking for. But if you do use reversals, you've lost the shadow side of the court card.

There really isn't a way to make a choice that doesn't limit you in some way. The reality is that you sacrifice something, no matter which way you go.

I use reversals with Marseille decks (though not with decks in the Waite-Smith tradition), but in working on this chapter, I've decided that the reversals option makes the most sense. I can tell from the overall message of the spread whether I'm dealing with the light or shadow aspect of someone's personality. Context makes it easier to detect whether the card is the client or someone in the client's life. Of the limited options, this is most elegant, most useful, and gives me something clear to work with. And even if I don't read reversals for the rest of the deck, I can still extract the courts, mix them up on the table in front of me, and slip them back into the deck before a good shuffle.

If ultimately you decide not to create a rule for the courts, then you really do have to use your intuition to tell you. And if you have strong psychic leanings, or just a really powerful ability to see who's who, then that won't be a problem for you. The rest of us will have to work a little harder.

In the past, I've solved that problem simply by explaining the card in both ways. "It could mean this, or it could mean that." Doing so has always made me uncomfortable, as though I should know the answer and I'm hedging my bets. But I've done that in other situations, too, not related to the courts. I've had to say, "I know you're asking about your work, but there are so many mother cards in this reading, I have to give you another way of looking at this." (Breaking my own rule, of course, about answering the question that was asked—but sometimes you do that. Nobody is going to call the tarot police on you. And hopefully no one calls the real police, either.)

Tarot is a human invention, and as such isn't perfect. And if you really wanted, and sometimes I think about doing this, you could just get two copies of the deck, take the courts out of the second, put a mark on each card, say that the cards with the mark represent the querent and the ones without represent other people. Technically that wouldn't be a traditional tarot deck, but who cares? If you care, then that's not the solution for you. If you don't, and you can afford it, why not?

Someday someone may provide me with the ideal solution. I clearly haven't found it. For the sake of the examples in the rest of the book, I'm going to use the reversed (client)/upright (other) method. That will keep things consistent, and you'll have a sense of why I'm interpreting things in the way I am. I'll talk about the good and the bad qualities of the court card equally, since most people aren't all one thing or another anyway. Then, I'll look for potential influence based on the cards around it. For your examples, feel free to do whatever feels right.

Once we wrestle with the demon of how to tell whether the courts are the clients or those in the client's life, we have a less frustrating task in front of us. Namely, exploring the character traits of the cards, in light and shadow, and the relationship of those traits to the elements.

In essence, we're building a matrix—or doing more math. Page traits + elemental traits = specific court card personality.

There are many ways to do this, up to and including using the Myers-Briggs Personality Type Indicators. But having a system that has already worked for us, we're going to forge ahead with it.

Activity 6.1: Starting from Scratch with the Courts

Objective: Refresh our view of the courts by thinking about them as a blank slate.

Why you should do this: The courts have accrued a lot of baggage over the centuries. Starting from zero allows us to refresh our method, clarify our readings, and re-engage with these sometimes puzzling cards.

Note: This is one of the few activities in the book that assumes you have a relationship to tarot already. If you don't, not to worry. Skip to step 2.

Instructions:

1. Consider everything you've learned about the court cards over the course of your reading life, and try to put it aside. Pretend as much as you can that these concepts are brand new, and allow yourself to be a curious student.

2. Using the small table below, think about each court position. (For the sake of clarity, I'm using the traditional English titles, rather than the French. Partly because we tend to talk about them using the English and partly because there are many variations in spelling and subtext for Marseille-style decks.) For each position, ask yourself what you know about it. Not about it in the context of tarot, but in historical context. What did that role do? Why? In relationship to whom? You may want to use a dictionary to start with the literal definition of each of these terms. Sometimes words get so used, and we get so used to them, that we forget what they actually mean. Make notes in the middle column.

3. Next, think about what relationship these concepts have to modern life. As always, there isn't a wrong answer. The aim is to start with the clearest definitions of what a page, knight, queen, and king

represent, and then connect those concepts to things as they are today. One of the goals of this is to shake the dust off words and statuses that don't really have much currency to people today. Who is a king in modern life? Not just in modern life, but *your* life. You likely don't have connection to a king day-to-day, so who would he be?

Here's an example, using another sort of dated historical role. Pretend for a moment that there is a tarot court card titled the Journeyman. Here's how that might go:

Journeyman

What it means: A day laborer. Someone who learned a trade through apprenticeship, and works for day-to-day wages. While the journey part of it didn't really relate to moving around, the word does give the feeling of someone who is nomadic or itinerant. Like a drifter or a wanderer. There's also a sense of hard labor or drudgery, according to Merriam-Webster.

How it could exist in modern life: This might be someone who moves from job to job a lot, who can't sit still, and who doesn't have specific long-term goals. Someone who works under the table, or follows seasonal work—like a farmer or fruit-picker. It's also used today to describe athletes, as well as directors of TV shows who aren't attached to a specific series. This person is likely rootless, and comfortable with that.

That's what we're going for. I chose a fake court card because it wouldn't be right to do your homework for you, though I will share my work with you later so that you can see what I came up with. In the meantime, it's off to work you go. Let me underscore again the importance of making your final summaries relevant to modern life. Too many readings could be so much more helpful if we as readers took the time to draw clearer, stronger lines between arcane archetypes and the lives we're leading today.

PAGE	
KNIGHT	
QUEEN	
KING	

Debrief: It can be both scary and exhilarating to start from scratch with the court cards. If we've never worked with them before, it is profoundly helpful to start with a strong foundation. Regardless of the system we ultimately use for the courts, it's important to remember that—royalty though they may be—the ultimate monarch is the reader. But in the absence of true leadership, the court will revolt and leave us scratching our heads—or losing them, entirely.

The next step in the process is to combine the court positions with the four elements, to explore how they depict sixteen different types of people, rather than four.

Activity 6.2: Court + Element

Objective: Connect the traits of the courts with the elements.

Why you should do this: To gain the full picture of the tarot court.

Instructions:
1. Using the table below, work on a pairing of each of the court cards to each of the elements. Like the work we did with the numbers and the elements, the aim is to create a relevant, active, and clear connection while recognizing that the meaning will evolve in the course of readings.
2. Note the "final" meaning in the final column.

For example, let's use the imaginary Journeyman card again.

Journeyman + Fire/Wands = a passionate drifter, who excites people's fancies before moving away; a ramblin' man; a creative person who moves where the work is; a revival minister.

Journeyman + Water/Cups = a romantic-but-rootless soul; a discontent, who can't settle down; a poet or bard; a guileless heartbreaker.

Journeyman + Air/Swords = a guest lecturer or educator who works as an adjunct; an investigative reporter; a self-help guru who travels from town to town.

Journeyman + Earth/Coins = a day laborer (literal journeyman); a derelict or absentee parent; a land prospector or even a slumlord.

I've gotten somewhat specific in my combos. In essence, my aim is to create modern archetypes—both light and shadow. I don't mean that were the "Journeyman of Coins" to show up in a reading I would necessarily be talking about a slumlord, but I would be talking about someone who has those traits generally. I'm trying to create a metaphor for the human experience, which is essentially what archetypes are. Thus, someone who found themselves locked in a business they can't afford or don't want to keep up (or both), someone who ignores the well-being of those who depend on him; or, conversely, someone whose duties keep them traveling and moving from place to place. But we'll get there in a bit. For now, on to the activity.

PAGE	**AIR**	
	FIRE	
	WATER	
	EARTH	
KNIGHT	**AIR**	
	FIRE	
	WATER	
	EARTH	
QUEEN	**AIR**	
	FIRE	
	WATER	
	EARTH	
KING	**AIR**	
	FIRE	
	WATER	
	EARTH	

Debrief: No matter how you feel about your combinations, you're closer to a realer, clearer, more modern interpretation of the courts.

The tarot was created in a world that no longer exists. While the archetypes that make up the trumps hold some currency for us today, it's not as much as it was when the game of tarot came to be. Think about how the decks created for the Visconti-Sforza families are believed to depict people from the families who commissioned those decks. It's unlikely those cards were used for divination, but even if they were, correspondences wouldn't have been hard to find. You wouldn't need to figure out what the King of Cups represented, you'd recognize Cousin Massimiliano and his tendency to spout off romantic poetry—and to get intoxicated at every evening meal. If the King of Cups came up, you'd know who you were talking about, or at least what kind of person he was.

Even once the cards jumped to France, the tarot court would have made sense. Knights and pages, by that time, may have gone the way of the dodo, true. But the French names for those cards, *chevalier* and *valet*, were current terms in the French court. And of course, everyone knew who the kings and queens were. The world has changed. Americans don't have a real relationship to kings, queens, and knights. Even the most famous monarch in the world, Queen Elizabeth II, serves a role dramatically different from that of her namesake. A king is not the same thing as a prime minister or president, and a queen is nobody's first lady. And even if they were, very few of us live in close proximity to heads of state for that to make sense. Kings and queens are our bosses and our parents; they're the people who have power in our lives.

Frankly, the principle difference is telling kings and queens apart, now. It could be gender, but that's equally outdated. Maybe we don't need both, but we have them. So, we work with them, and it gives us four more colors in the reading.

Here's how I see them:

Kings are our bosses, our leaders, the gatekeepers of our goals; they're the people we aspire to be, or the part of ourselves others aspire to. They are the most experienced at what they do, and have the most knowledge of it.

Queens are our mentors, our enablers, our benefactors; they're the producers, the commissioners, the therapists, the guides. They are the people who help us achieve our goals, who we go to for advice. Or, they're us when we're doing that for others.

Knights are verbs. They are the doers, seekers, hunters. They're going out and making their way. They're restless, active, motivated, and ambitious. They're the go-getters, and, of course, us when we're out there going and getting.

Pages are students. They're curious; they're inspired and interested. They're novices. They're us at the beginning of journeys, with our fascination piqued and our slate clean. They're our children, our protégés, our students, our employees, and our dependents. They are those who look up to us. We are who they want to be.

Nobody in the court is royal; all of them are us.

It's worth pausing here to discuss gender. In my practice, I have stripped gender away from the court cards. Each represents all genders. In the evolution of my approach to the courts, I wrestled for a long time with the inevitably sexist correspondence of the queens. Not everyone gets to sit at the top of the ladder, and kings have traditionally played that role. The monarchy is inherently patriarchal; the tarot, which came out of monarchal societies, tends to be, too. I resisted making the queen a nurturer, because that felt too easy, too stereotypical. I couldn't reconcile it any other way, though, and eventually gave in. Because I don't view the courts as any sex, I reluctantly allow it to be what it is. But it is frustrating, even when, say, the pages become princesses. The ladies always wind up in a secondary role. Until someone comes up with a solution, do what you want with them. Flip the kings and the queens. Make the kings enablers and the queens rulers. Who cares? You get to decide. Tony DiMauro, creator of *The Darkness of Light* tarot, put the queens at the top. As long as you know what you mean when you see them, as long as the tarot knows your rules, it can be whatever you want. And I say go for it.

Let's take this all a step further, though, because I really want you to have a deep enough connection to the courts that you don't feel a moment of anxiety when you see them. We'll do that through another activity.

Activity 6.3: Who's Who in the Court?

Objective: Further solidify the tarot court as people in our lives.

Why you should do this: The clearer and more grounded the tarot court is to humanity, the easier it will be to read them and the sharper your readings will be.

Instructions:

1. Below, you'll find a table with a list of all sixteen tarot courts. The middle column is titled "celebrity," and the last column is titled "acquaintance." The task is simple. Think about the qualities of that court card, and then think of a celebrity who most embodies those qualities. They can be modern or historical, politician, entertainer, etc. Someone well-known in your eyes who "is" that court.

2. Take a break.

3. Return, and repeat in the final column. This time, you're thinking of people you know, people in your life, who you have met and spent time with. It could be anyone from anywhere in your personal history, but someone you've known at least well enough to see them as one of these cards.

COURT	CELEBRITY	ACQUAINTENCE
PAGE OF WANDS		
KNIGHT OF WANDS		
QUEEN OF WANDS		
KING OF WANDS		
PAGE OF CUPS		
KNIGHT OF CUPS		
QUEEN OF CUPS		

KING OF CUPS		
PAGE OF SWORDS		
KNIGHT OF SWORDS		
QUEEN OF SWORDS		
KING OF SWORDS		
PAGE OF COINS		
KNIGHT OF COINS		
QUEEN OF COINS		
KING OF COINS		

Debrief: Since our aim is not only to read pip decks, like Tarot de Marseille, but to bring our readings into sharp, practical focus, this activity helps us ground the tarot. By equating each of the courts with a famous personality as well as someone in our own history, we continue to build a deeper, richer, more useful experience of those court cards. That means their appearance in readings will be deeper, richer, and more useful, too. It is fine, for example, to say, when the Queen of Swords appears, "Oh, gosh, you know who this woman is—she's Martha Stewart!" Just for example. And, of course, everyone has different experiences of celebrities and Aunt Judy, so that must be accounted for. But because you view Martha Stewart as a sharp, smart, fierce enabler of skill and talent, who can also sometimes be cutting, you have a sense of how those qualities exist in life. Because you know Aunt Judy is practical to a fault, generous, earthy, hearty, dutiful, and tends to put others before herself to the point that she's developed a martyr complex and a hole in her bank account, you have a real-life experience of the Queen of Coins. You may not want to tell Martha Stewart or Aunt Judy that they modeled those traits, but it's going to be an incredible mnemonic for readings.

It's possible that you now have a deeper relationship with the "minor arcana" than I had for most of my reading life. It's also odd, now, how in the context of this course, calling these cards the minor arcana feels off. There's nothing minor or arcane about these cards, and that's the very reason we're starting here. Nearly every book I've ever encountered on tarot puts the trumps, the major arcana, first. And we will, I promise, dig into the majors in a juicy and cool way and put all the pieces together. But by going so deeply into the pips and the courts, we've given them their due respect. As I've said before, these cards collectively make up what happens in our daily lives and the people with whom we share that. Our larger journeys in life are still important, but life demands of us that we spend most of our time dealing with banalities. That's not bad. If we spent every hour of every day with our eyes trained on the spiritual quest, we'd go mad. And, frankly, doing that with the phone ringing and TV to watch seems nearly impossible.

Which brings up an interesting question—if you had to think of a card right now that represented the phone ringing or a text message, what would it be? What about a TV show we want to watch? What do you think? Take a second before looking at what I chose, in the footnote.[2]

Tackling questions like that and journaling about them can take your practice even deeper. I can't remember a time I gave a reading and saw the Five of Swords as phone calls or texts. It's unlikely I'd discover that, unless I designed or used a deck with that image on the card. But the associations I've worked up for it are, in part, "disrupted communication." It's not a far walk to "disruptive communication." If I'm reading for someone who wants to know why they can't get anything done, and I'm looking at the Five of Swords, my inner monologue could easily take me there. If disruptive communication clicks, then I think about what forms of communication can be disruptive, and I immediately think of social networking, phone, and text. Especially since our phones are essentially built for the purpose of distracting us.

So far we've looked at the pips and we've looked at the court cards, but we haven't yet put them together. In this next activity, the time has come to do that. I truly recommend committing to a consistent method of describing whether a court is the client or someone in the client's life—even if only for this practice. Doing so will make your head hurt less, and may actually show you that though choosing a method involves sacrificing something, you gain a kind of clarity you haven't had before. Again, for the purpose of my example below, I'm using reversed courts to represent the client and upright courts to represent people influencing the client. (I've used this method in the past few days, as I've worked on this

2   Phone or text interruptions would be the Five of Swords, in my world—since air represents communication, and five represents disruption. A TV show seducing me away from my work is tougher. But I think the Nine of Wands reversed—my interest in something pulling me way from getting work done.

chapter, and I have to say the only thing I dislike about it is extracting all the courts for decks I don't read reversals with and mixing them up. But in the scheme of things? Not too bad.)

Activity 6.4: Court in the Act

Objective: To incorporate the courts into readings with the pips.

Why you should do this: This will take all the work you've done with the courts so far, and bring it to life. It'll also further your connection with the rest of the pips.

Instructions:

1. Put about twenty of the pips into a pile. It doesn't matter which ones or what suit they are. Ideally a few from each suit.
2. Take all sixteen of the court cards. If you're joining me in using reversed and upright cards to differentiate the courts, mix them up now.
3. Shuffle your twenty pips and sixteen court cards.
   a. We're working with only twenty of the pips purely to increase the likelihood of courts showing up in the spreads.
4. Use this short stack to perform three nine-card readings on the following questions. As always, I recommend recording your work, your "math," for future reference.
   a. Note that nine cards can be time-consuming, but of course it's practice doing something we love. If you use a six- or

three-card reading, have a sense of how you'll read the spread beforehand. That way you won't feel stumped. For example, if you choose a six-card spread, two lines of three, you might decide ahead of time that you're going to read the cards in rows of three and columns of two. Knowing what you're going to do before you do it helps tell the cards and your brain what to expect, and stops you from feeling confused after the cards are laid out.

1. What is the best way to improve my happiness at work?
2. How can I catch Steve's attention?
3. What's really wrong with my relationship?
4. What does she really think of me?

Debrief: Limiting the number of total pips for the exercise served no other purpose than to increase the potential appearance of court cards. The process of reading should have been no different, and hopefully you feel more confident in working with the courts in a reading.

My try:

Question: What does she really think of me?

Inner monologue/my math: Right out of the gate I'm looking for the court cards, and which ones are my client and which are someone else. Because he's asking about "her," I'm going to assume most, if not all, of the up

right cards represent her. The Page of Cups reversed and the Knight of Swords reversed are him. Immediately, I could say she thinks he's smart and ambitious but is emotionally juvenile. In a way, those two cards tell me everything, but I drew nine so I have to work with nine. And that's a good thing, because I can look for evidence. Camelia Elias recommends using the reading to find evidence for the interpretation we come up with. This is a rare time where I got an answer that quickly, so it's most definitely worth looking for evidence.

First, let's look at how she's depicted: King of Wands and Queen of Swords. She's likely older than he, if we think about courts as a progression of experience. But even if she's not, she's definitely more mature. He's depicted in the reading by two "youth" cards, she's two "adult" cards. What I know about her is that she's intensely passionate and not opposed to initiating others (King of Wands), and that she's smart and a good guide. So, his inexperience may not be an issue for her. And this is why evidence is so important, because if I'd stopped with my initial thought, I would have said, "she thinks you're smart but emotionally immature." That's not quite the language I'd use at this point.

I also see that they're both represented by swords cards, so even though she's probably more experienced than he, they do have an intellectual connection and that's good.

Now that I've got a sense of them as people, let me explore the reading using all the cards.

Row 1: A spark of passion makes an inexperienced lover willing to earn his keep.

Row 2: An experienced, passionate superior feels a growing connection, but she also has some long-standing views or values that are preventing her from being super interested in shaking things up.

Row 3: There's still work to do between a smart, restless go-getter and a smart, experienced mentor.

Column 1: A passionate spark exists for a passionate and experienced person who sees that relationships take time and effort.

Column 2: That inexperienced lover/smart, ambitious thinker is feeling all kinds of things growing inside him.

Column 3: It's going to take a lot of effort, a lot of work, for that smart, experienced mentor to get over her preconceived notions about how things should work.

If you're curious about how I wound up with the explanations of the rows, go back and look at my interpretations of the numbers and elements. Just to give you a clue, though, I went a bit rogue with the Ten of Coins reversed. Since ten is completion and coins is work, duty, responsibility, etc., I decided that it meant "unfinished work" in its reversed mode. As such, it became a symbol of something good—effort continuing—rather than something bad.

I've got a lot of information here. Sharing it all might be helpful to my client. But first, let me focus on the important thing: answering the question he asked.

Final answer: She thinks you're maybe a little inexperienced, but she's not turned off by that. She might enjoy helping you grow.

* * *

That's the salient point. Everything else is gravy, and I can share it with him: she can be a bit stuck in her ways, so it's going to take some work to convince her; there's work to be done between you, and it's not the sexy work, it's the practical work. I can share all of that. But I need to make sure the thing he remembers most is the answer to the question he asked.

One thing I haven't talked much about is the importance of feedback. How do we know if we're doing something right unless there's feedback? We don't. And it's hard to give feedback when we're not sitting together. On the other hand, in order for me to give you really great feedback I'd have to internalize all your learnings with you. So even if we were sitting together, I'd need you to walk me through how you landed on what you did.

Absent that, the best way to get feedback on these exercises is to check yourself against the question that you were answering. Did you answer the question? Or, did you go off on a tangent that gave access to all the brilliant wisdom you learned from the reading, but that did not answer the question? That's the best way to discover how well you're doing.

You may argue that the *best* way to check yourself is finding out whether your answer is right or wrong. A lot of us worry about that when we do readings. Was I right on? Did I get what I was supposed to? Does that sound right? We can't get that in practice readings, but guess what? We may or may not get it in real readings, either. In the example I did above, the only way I could know whether I was right or wrong was if this woman were available for a consultation. My client might agree or disagree, but all I can do is work out what I work out. And even if the reading were about him, I could say, "you're all these things" and he could turn around and say, "no, I'm not!" What then? We're done. We don't always see ourselves as we really are, and if we don't, we're not likely to let cards tell us things about ourselves we don't want to know.

We create brands, impressions of ourselves that we're selling to the larger world around us. We don't like when people tell us we're off-brand or that we're engaging in false advertising. So even when a client tells me I'm wrong, or that I'm spot on, I never really know if that's true. They may think I'm spot on because they like what I said, because I said something they interpreted as a compliment, or when I pointed to the Knight of Cups and said, "that's you," they thought, "damn, I look hot in that picture!"

The best way to check yourself is to look at whether or not you provided an answer to the question that is actually an answer to the question, and not a soliloquy of brilliant but disparate and verbose commentaries on the cards.

That brings us to the end of this section. Before we move on, are you feeling discouraged at all? Do you feel as though you're not closer to more grounded readings than you were before? Are you still resisting the charms of working with non-situational pip cards? If that's the case, that's OK. Nothing about what we do is easy, and even when it is easy, it's generally not easy all the time. Whatever the level of difficulty, though, it should be enjoyable. Let's take a pulse check and see how we're doing. Take a moment and answer the following questions:

1. Have you been doing the activities, as written?

2. Have you been taking breaks?
3. Have you *really* been doing the activities?
4. Have you *really* been taking breaks?
5. Are you skipping the messy part, in which you do the math—where you work through the array of possible meanings and create associations?
6. How clear are your numerological, elemental, and court associations?
7. How current are your references?

Questions three and four may seem like I'm trying to be cute. I'm not. Experts in learning have convinced me that these things are essential. Practice and allow yourself time to rest. That combination is necessary in sports, so that athletes don't get injured. It's essential in this, so that we truly internalize the lessons.

Nothing about this is a science. If only it were as clear as math, right? Of course, if it were, anyone could do it and we'd all do it the same way, and who would need to study it?

This pulse check isn't about perfectionism. It's about sitting with ourselves and exploring what we've done thus far. It's another kind of break.

So here are some remedies:
1. If you haven't done the activities fully, go back and do them as written.
2. If you haven't taken breaks, go back and review the work you did. Study it, like you might for a test. Then test yourself. How well are

you remembering what you learned?

3. Do the activities again.

4. Spend time in the messy part; allow yourself to get in the dirt. Nobody but you will ever see what you write here, so don't be afraid to come to conclusions that you would never settle on. Each unexpected insight is still an insight that could yield something good.

5. Review your summaries of the numbers, elements, and courts. Try to find clearer, more active words.

6. Don't give up.

Having come this far, it's not worth giving up. You've invested a lot. I mean, let's be honest. I've put you through the ringer. Check in with yourself. Are you tired? If so, go read something else and come back to this in a week. For real. Are you feeling energized? If so, let's forge ahead.

And, as ever, this as an opportunity to check yourself against your goals. How has what you've developed helped you come closer to your tarot progress?

◊ Interlude 3: Intuition ◊

The words "intuition" and "intuitive" get bandied around a lot in our community. Ain't nothing wrong with that, in my opinion, other than the inevitable: words that we use a lot tend after a while to stop having any meaning. It's not anything bad; it's just the curse of familiarity.

Have you ever read a book and found an unfamiliar word you really liked? In context, you knew exactly what the author meant. You knew without having to reach for the dictionary what it meant. And being a good word nerd, you immediately incorporated it into your lexicon. Nobody questioned it, because why would they? Its meaning is so precise it defies definition. Until one day one brave soul says, "what's *that* mean?" And, faced suddenly with a need to express its meaning, you have no idea how to define it.

Words are funny.

I bring this up mostly to justify our own relationship to the intuition-based words we use in tarot. There's never been any real reason to define them for each other, because we all know what they mean. We've read the same books, we've participated in the same forums and chats, we know what we mean.

Except, do we? It's possible we don't.

There are those who view "intuitive reading" as the act of laying out and listening to the cards. There are others who view it as "lazy," i.e., a refusal to learn the "real" meanings of the cards. (Who gets to define the real meanings? Generally, whoever thinks that cards have "real" meanings.)

Allow me to take you on a journey into my theories about intuition. It's important to know that, unlike my theories on adult learning and tarot itself, these are not based on research. These are based, well, on intuition.

What do you see in the figure, below?

Don't overthink it; this isn't anything complicated. Hopefully you see a rectangle. Me, too.

What about this?

And this?

And, finally, this.

These are shapes we recognize, because we learned them at a young age—but also because we're surrounded by them. Everything around us is some variation or mutation of these shapes, and combinations of these shapes. Our brain recognizes shapes, and the combination of shapes in context tells us something.

You're doing it right now. Each word on this page is made up of shapes. We know the meaning of those shapes, because we learned them, and we learned that in combination the shapes become words, and the words become meaningful. We also learned that many of those combinations of shapes have multiple meanings. We learned that when words are gathered into sentences, the combination of those words in a sentence will narrow down a word's potential meaning. Even though the meaning of the words evolves over time, the context allows us to figure out the meaning. "Shoot me an e-mail," a common phrase in modern offices, has nothing to do with guns.

That we can read, or listen, and make sense of anything is because our brains are designed to recognize patterns—not only recognize them, but seek them out. Patterns are how we make sense of the world. We know that the pattern of cars driving slowly means we may want take an alternate route. We know that the pattern of coughing, sneezing, and congestion means that we have a cold. The letter Q alone means very little, in the same way a single blink of the eye means nothing. The letter Q in the context of the letters U, E, S, and T tells us we're going on a journey. The fluttering of an eyelash means there's something stuck in our eye.

Patterns are another form of context that teach us about the world. From the sound of stampeding bison, to the combination of tomato sauce, cheese, dough, and pepperoni, patterns tell us what we should be afraid of and what we can expect for dinner.

To take it further, we don't just recognize the pattern of tomato sauce, cheese, dough, and pepperoni; we know that all of those things are edible, and we know that they are collectively called pizza. If the combo were tomatoes sauce, dough, cheese, and plastic soldiers, we would know we don't have pizza—or we would know at least that one of these things is not like the others.

Not only can we recognize the pattern that makes up pizza, we can communicate that entire combination by calling it "pizza." Many people will instantly understand what we mean. All of this because of patterns.

 What I'm getting at, ultimately, is that intuition can be easily explained in part as our ability to recognize patterns. Leaving behind an actual psychic ability to know things are happening without having any relationship to them, most of the things we sense with our intuition are the result of observing patters.

"I have a feeling that marriage isn't going to last." Why? Because I've noticed tiny little glances between them; little snarky comments that seemed to be jokes, but happened too frequently not to have some deeper meaning; Jennifer's enthusiasm about Tom was *far* too gushing at lunch the other day. They aren't fighting. No one's cheating on the other. Still, the sense that the marriage isn't going to last is pervasive, and it's because of the recognition of subtle patterns that allow us to draw a conclusion.

Whether it's a political event, someone's ability to do a job, or what we'll get for a birthday gift, our intuition is largely empowered by patterns that we're picking up on, whether or not we notice it. The old sitcom joke of "women's intuition" was based on the stereotype that women are more observant than men. Which make sense, because the world is patriarchal and as such straight, white men didn't need to navigate a world that put them in danger. Women lived in a world of varying degrees of danger that required a greater awareness of their surroundings, a greater need to watch and observe patterns.

I recognize I'm wading into tricky political waters. My point is that everyone has access to this kind of intuition, because it's innate. People have commented on my own intuitive ability, or my insight into people's psyches. I can tell a lot about people I don't know, and I generally have a good sense of their ticks and especially their insecurities. I intuit, accurately, a lot about people shortly after meeting them, and the more I get to know them, the more I seem to be able to explain their behavior. I don't have any special training in psychology. My degree is in writing.

But growing up constantly in danger of being beaten up because I was a nerdy, bookish, effeminate child meant that I had to learn as much about other people as quickly as possible in order to protect myself. Was this person a threat? Were they someone who might attack? Were they an ally? I needed to find this out to limit the chances of getting smacked around. I grew insightful because I had to be.

If "Sitcom Husband" was living in the woods and survived on what he killed, he would likely be far more intuitive than Donna Reed. Conditioning affects the natural intuition we use on a daily basis. If threats are greater, we are more intuitive. And the kind of intuition we exhibit will depend on what our threats are. A city-dweller is far more likely to sense an unseen car speeding down the street than a visitor to the city, because the city-dweller's ears are tuned to the sound. It's a threat they're looking out for. A farm-dweller may know that foxes are in the area without seeing them, because they recognize the behavior of the chickens—something a city-dweller might never notice.

Having an awareness of the kinds of intuition our conditions have given us access to can go a long away in our tarot practice. It also helps us recognize that we have it at all.

These interludes are meant to give you a break from the activities, but you might, if you were of a mind, pause and think about the kinds of intuition you have developed in your life. An easy way to start that is to think about where you grew up and the kinds of threats that might have been around you. When I say threats, I mean things that could have caused danger—so it could be cars or bears; I'm not necessarily talking about dangerous tempers of relatives. Still, that is part of your makeup, and, sadly, you will have learned to recognize people's mood-triggers in an effort to survive, so that will be part of this, too. What are the things you seem to know or at least sense without obvious clues, and what life conditions do you think allowed you to exercise that part of your intuition? Journal about it, if you want.

This is all by way of saying that everyone has intuition, because it's part of the survival skills animals are born with. Our life conditions have allowed us to access parts of it, but not all of it. Still, even if we lived an incredibly sheltered life, without fear of threat, the ability is still there because we can recognize patterns. We can read, we can write, we can talk and hear and understand.

Consider the shapes from earlier:

What do you see?

Shapes, a circle, square, rectangle, and triangle. You can see that the triangle's point is upside down, which may be unusual or unexpected. This pattern tells us "shapes," it may say "geometry," or "school" or any number of associations we have with primary shapes such as these.

Now, let's reorder them. This is something I've seen on a popular bumper sticker.

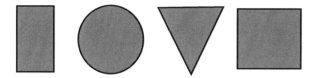

Shapes, still. But see anything else?

The world LOVE, maybe? Even if you didn't see it, now you probably will—because you've learned it. And now it's hard to un-see.

This is just another example of our brain's ability to recognize patterns. From words to shapes to the Magic Eye posters of the 1990's, we are built to see and recognize patterns, give them meaning, and communicate that meaning.

We may not all have accessed this skill as actively in our lives as others, but we all possess it. That means, regardless of who we are and what our experience is, we can learn to do this. We can learn to read cards. It is not an activity limited to those who were born intuitive. It is limited only to those who are willing to develop their intuition. Like all things, there will be adepts. Some people are gifted with access to deeper ability in certain things than other. Some people can hit a baseball 500 feet. Most of us will never do that. That doesn't mean we can't learn to hit a baseball, and that doesn't mean we can learn to hit a home run. Most of us will never paint the Mona Lisa, but the real gap between being a painter and not is the willingness to pick up a paint brush.

Famed 1970's PBS icon, painter, and general decent human Bob Ross said that talent is nothing more than applied interest. He meant that you don't get good at stuff unless you have an interest and then do it. Julia Child, another of the heroes of my youth, encouraged her audience to get in the damn kitchen and make a mess. She learned how to make omelets by making a lot of shitty omelets. She became expert. And she still got on TV and screwed it up sometimes and told us to throw some parsley on it. Bob Ross and Julia Child were brilliant teachers, because they didn't take these arts—painting and French food, two things typically associated with elitists—and make them impossible. They told us to get in the sandbox and make a mess, and to keep doing that, and if we were really willing to do that over and over, we could get good at it. We may never end up Caravaggio or Escoffier, but we *will* get good at it.

One of the things that keeps people from pursuing anything is the idea of genius. "I'm not a genius. I'll never be that good." They never try, or they give up when it gets too hard. Elizabeth Gilbert, in her book *Big Magic*, reminds us that there was a time in history when a genius was not something you were; it was something you were visited by. Meaning that genius came, muse-like, and graced you with its presence. When genius visited, everything just *worked.* And then it went away, and things went back to normal—i.e., they got harder again. This is helpful to remember, because it makes everything feel more possible. There *will* be readings that are beautiful, effortless, and insanely insightful. They will trip off the tongue and electrify the querent and everything will feel magical and you'll recognize yourself as the sage you always wanted to be. And then there will be readings where looking at the cards feels like rubbing your eyes with sandpaper, and you wonder why you ever picked them up to begin with. Reading will be a struggle, and you will feel totally insecure in your interpretation. And then, most times, you'll feel something in between. And that's OK. That's human. That's how it's supposed to feel.

But one thing is certain, if you apply your interest—if you make it your business to practice and connect—you will come closer to those magic times more frequently. You will open up and exercise your intuition, or at least the version of it I've explored above, and you will get better. That's a sure bet.

PART II:
THE TRUMPS

◊ The Trumps ◊

I wrestled with what to call the different parts of the deck throughout this course. I'm not wild about the word "trump" at the moment, for reasons I won't bother elaborating on. At the same time, I'm not especially wild about "major arcana." I've avoided as much as I could so far using the terms major and minor arcana, because in a sense, I'm attempting to turn the clock back a bit before the Golden Dawn "rectified" the deck. I want to reiterate that I don't have an issue with the Golden Dawn system, and certainly not the Waite-Smith tradition. I adore Pamela Colman Smith's drawings, and her majors are a true work of art. Her whole deck was clearly visited by genius, especially given how quickly she created it. When asked to choose my favorite Fool, Magician, Empress, and Hermit cards, her drawings are the ones I reach for.

The Golden Dawn gave us tarot as we know it today. The French esotericists who followed de Gebelin, Eteilla in particular, certainly developed the tarot tradition. But had the Golden Dawn not formed in London in the late 19th century, it's impossible to imagine what the modern tarot landscape might look like. I don't believe that we never would have discovered tarot as a tool. Lenormand Cards were nowhere in the American landscape about six or eight years ago. Now, they're incredibly popular. Tarot would likely have followed a similar path. But when Arthur Edward Waite learned of the tarot through the Golden Dawn and decided that it needed to be corrected, he set off a chain reaction that continues to this day. Many, many of us wouldn't be engaged in this tarot world had Waite not felt compelled to publish his deck. Even Aleister Crowley, whose deck has landed in our midst as a result of the Golden Dawn, would likely not have had the influence he did.

Tarot readers in the English-speaking world owe a debt to the Hermetic Order of the Golden Dawn, who took the work of Court de Gebelin, Eteilla, Papus, Lévi, and others, and codified it into a formal system. Beyond that, they also gave the world Arthur Edward Waite, Pamela Colman Smith, Aleister Crowley, and Lady Frieda Harris. Those folks were only too eager to share what they'd discovered in the Golden Dawn and share it with the larger world.

The Golden Dawn gets a lot of credit for providing the esoteric relationship between the tarot and Kabbalah, astrology, alchemy, etc. The reality is that Eteilla's earliest cartomantic readings may have had a connection to at least Kabbalistic numerology, though he may not have known it. Ronald Decker in *The Esoteric Tarot: Ancient Sources Rediscovered in Hermeticism and Cabalah* compares Eteilla's cartomantic meanings for the pips (and playing cards) with the work of Spanish cabalist Joseph Ben Abraham Gikatilla. It's possible Eteilla may not have known he was borrowing these meanings, but having developed them by interviewing older cartomancers, he picked them up nonetheless. Eteilla was also the first person to link the elements with the pips, though Lévi later switched the association of coins and wands to that which we're most familiar with today.

Later occultists didn't really care about the pips—even though, according to Decker, they borrowed liberally from Eteilla's work on them. The "greater trumps" or "major arcana" were more important. Those cards held the secrets of lost knowledge. What occultists cared about was mysticism. And from the moment Court de Gebelin proclaimed the tarot a divinatory tool, the aim was primarily to demonstrate the cards' relationship to the spiritual paths of the thinkers who took it up. In a way, tarot is by default an esoteric tool, purely because we have no evidence that anyone before the French occultists used it for anything other than a game. But cartomancy, before and after the revelation by Court de Gebelin, existed in less spiritual, less philosophical circles. The earliest human cultures used pictures to convey meanings, and we know that from the Oracle at Delphi to the tossing of bones and dice, people have used whatever systems they could think of to intuit the meaning of things and predict the potential. From the studying of animal entrails to the Doppler Radar, humans are by nature disposed to looking at patterns and finding answers in them.

Frankly, I think history has preferred the esoteric approach to tarot because of its patriarchal bent. History's occultists were mostly men—certainly the names we recall today were—and the "folk magicians" who would have used more practical divination tools were women. These are the same women who delivered the children and cured with herbs; the same women who would have been burned at the stake had a rich man's cows suddenly died. Mademoiselle Marie Lenormand had been almost entirely ignored by history until recently, and it has been women like Mary K. Greer, Rana George, Donnaleigh Delarosa who have resurrected her place in the history of cartomancy.[1] Even Eteilla, a man, was discredited by later occultists as something of a hack—and they discredited him in part by noting that he was a *hairdresser.* We recognize the stereotypical effeminacy of that profession, don't we? "*That* man? But he was just a *hairdresser!*" And while Eteilla provided the groundwork for the card meanings that would come through Waite's deck and into our modern books, Lévi and others used a rumor of a womanly profession to discredit his work (while appropriating what they wanted).

I bring this up here in particular because the trumps are the cards most affected by the patina of esoteric thinking. In the years since Court de Gebelin declared them the book of all human knowledge, each generation has painted their esoteric needs onto the cards. Hundreds of years later, the trumps can appear waxy with age and hazy with philosophy. Many people have found lots of those layers helpful, otherwise tarot wouldn't have survived. Still, I find the trumps frequently more difficult to interpret than the pips because of the heady philosophies applied to them—systems that seem to have little relationship to modern life.

....

1   In fairness, Michael Dummet, Ronald Decker, and Theirry Depaulis dedicate a great deal of attention to her in their book, *A Wicked Pack of Cards: Origins of the Occult Tarot* (1996). Though until the sudden explosion of Lenormand card reading in the past decade, she was largely ignored. Granted, she was not a tarot reader, so her work didn't fall into the scope of most books. However, she fits into the pantheon of women in history who did remarkable things only to have their work eclipsed by the men.

Ronald Decker, in *The Esoteric Tarot*, argues that there is some evidence to suggest that there are ancient mysteries folded into the tarot deck. While his scholarship is rich and thoughtful, I'm not yet sold. The links still feel co-incidental (I chose that spelling carefully), and the many variations on what became tarot throughout world history are so diverse and disconnected that I can't wrap my mind around there being any actual relationship. The relationship to cabalistic numerology is uncanny, but humanity seems to be naturally drawn to certain collections of numbers. The co-incidence may not be random but has more to do with the larger interconnectedness of everything in the universe than anything as small as a pack of cards.

I never want to denigrate the belief systems of others. As I said, people have found incredible meaning in the connection of the cards—the trumps in particular—to mystery traditions, and to that end, I say it's a success. There are others of us who have stared at the trump cards and had a sense of what they mean in the grander scheme of things, but have a hard time bringing that into any practical lesson. And why can't tarot be both a tool for spiritual exploration *and* a method of solving life's daily problems? Learning the esoteric traditions of the trumps doesn't mean that one can't also explore more down-to-earth meanings. Clearly the tarot is strong enough to support both.

The aim throughout this book is to bring the tarot down to earth, and so this exploration of the trumps will focus on doing just that. I prefer the Marseille-style trumps for these activities purely because they predate the active attempts to "rectify" them. Waite and Smith completely revolutionized the trumps—they were, of course, Waite's principle concern—and in doing, they began the process of lacquering the images with magic and alchemy. But in the images of the Marseille, it's easier to see the banal-but-beautiful body under the esoteric clothing.

Allow me one more digression before we get to the lessons. Much is made of finding the "true" meanings of the cards. All cartomantic traditions have a love affair with history. When history isn't available to those traditions, we simply make those histories up (I'm looking at you, Court de Gebelin). Whether one is an occultist or a practical fortune teller, we tend to treat card reading in part as an archeological act. Attempts to reach the "pure" or the "real" origin, meaning, and use of the cards has dominated discussions from the start. Tarot may be the champion, but I see this likewise in Lenormand, as well in books on reading playing cards.

Knowing the history is useful, particularly to those of us who eat up books on what interests us faster than they can be written. It's helpful to know how meanings developed and the contexts from which they emerged. But whether we're using folk magic or ceremonial magic, we have to wrestle with the inevitable fact: the traditions from which the cards emerged don't reflect the lives we're leading today.

Let's consider that great standard-bearer of decks, the Waite-Smith Tarot. While the situational pips revolutionized reading, the meanings that Smith depicts have everything to do with the cartomantic tradition that came before it. Kelly Fitzgerald, author and artist of *The Story in Color Lenormand*, has talked many times about how the Smith pips reflect a tradition in which the wands and the swords represent difficulties. Ronald Decker notes this as coming from the Eteilla cartomantic tradition, which seems to have had at least a tangential relationship to early cabalistic numerology. The swords and wands represent losses and challenges; the cups and coins represent happier things. If you've any familiarity with the Waite-Smith suit of swords, you can see off the bat what a disagreeable collection of images that suit is. The suit of spades has long had to do with death, disease, and struggle. Jonathan Dee's modern book, *Fortune Telling Using Playing Cards,* explores these meanings in more detail, as he looks at different traditions of reading playing cards.

Any good card slinger, regardless of their chosen deck or system, will have a balance of positive and negative in their meanings—light and shadow, as we call it here. Assigning the suits to positive and negative aspects of life provides a certain kind of balance. But let's consider that Eteilla also assigned each suit to the elements of fire, water, air, and earth. These elements are far more complicated than simply "losses and challenges." Water can both clean and destroy. Earth can be both fertile and barren. Fire can destroy but also cleans and creates. And it is literally impossible to breathe without air, while it can also intoxicate. Like most things, our relationship to those elements has changed over time. Ancients believed that these elements affected our temperament, as they were tied to the "humors" that made up our bodies. We've come to see the elements in modern life as both more literal and more figurative. Science has changed how we think about what makes us up; psychology has changed how we think about what we think, do, feel, and say. I have no evidence that Eteilla's elemental associations *didn't* apply to the cards as he saw them, but I can see without the need for any scholarship that the elements today don't reflect the suit associations of 17th and 18th century French card reading.

The world has changed. Life expectations have increased. How we view the world, how we view what scares and inspires us, all of those things are different than when Eteilla worked on his books. So finding the "true" meaning of the cards may be an interesting academic exercise, but the discovery of anything we might call the original meanings of the cards doesn't do much for the modern reader. We have to explore the cards in the context of the world we're living with today. To be a truly effective reader, I believe, we have to strip away hundred-year-old interpretations. Or, to think about it another way, we have to draw clearer lines between those old pictures and the world we're living in now.

With that in mind, we can proceed to exploring the trumps from a modern point of view.

Lesson 7:
◊ The Trumps in ◊
Real Life

Activity 7.1: Back to Life, Back to Reality

Objective: Connect the archetypes of the trumps with modern life.

Why you should do this: As discussed in the previous section, the trumps in particular have been lacquered year after year with arcane meanings and esoteric interpretations. Readings the cards in this way has been helpful to many. But exploring the cards in a different way can yield the kind of clear, practical, useful readings we're focused on in these pages.

Note: This activity should take a fair amount of time. For that reason, you have my permission (as though you need it) to work on this while you work on other activities in the book. Don't rush through this. Try to avoid settling. Enjoy this process, and let it take as long as it takes. And don't worry about going in order. When you find what you're looking for, take it—even if it doesn't follow the order of the trumps.

Instructions:

1. Using whatever deck you're focusing on, spend an hour or so exploring the trumps. The order doesn't matter. Just explore the images and think about what they mean to you. Think about all the things you've learned about them to date, if you've learned anything at all about them. If you haven't learned anything about them, think about what the title and picture tell you. Feel free to read some descriptions of the meanings from the little white book or guidebook that came with your deck. Consider how those images connect to the meanings you know or have researched.

2. Go out into the world. Anywhere you'd like: the mall, the park, school, anywhere. Look around you. Find the trumps in real life and take a picture of those trumps with your camera or phone. Here's the key, though. You're not looking for pictures that look like the images on the card; you're looking for experiences that embody the card's meaning as you understand it. For example, coming across two people looking up at the angel of Bethesda Fountain in Central Park may look to you like the Lovers card, but does it express what you *feel* about the card? Instead, you come across a man texting furiously on the phone while his girlfriend tries to get his attention. That's more an embodiment of the Lovers from a Marseille-style deck, from my perspective. You're attempting to capture the es-

sence of the card in life. Happening on a drunken tantrum in a bar is more The Devil than a group of trick-or-treaters dressed like demons—unless, of course, those trick-or-treaters begging for candy say "the devil" to you.

3. Repeat for all twenty-two of the trumps, including the Fool.
4. If you've got the resources, print them and make a photo album or a notebook that you can continue adding to over time.

Note: Most tarot readers long to create their own deck, and many of us lack the artistic ability to do it. If you decide during this project that your photos would make a great deck, please consider the rights of others. If you're going to use images you've taken of people you don't know, they deserve the right to accept or decline that opportunity. If you do decide to publish pictures, ask the subjects to sign a waiver and respect their wishes if they say no. Social networks and smart phones have taken a great deal of our agency away when it comes to how images of us are used. People become memes against their will, and that can, in some cases, ruins lives. Don't contribute to that unfortunate development. Allow people the right to make the choice. This could cramp your style as you work on this activity, so I recommend putting the experience of the lesson before thinking of using these images for anything else.

Alternatives: If you find yourself homebound or nervous about going out into the world to do this activity, then I recommend taking advantage of the news. Using newspapers, television news, magazines, the internet, etc., cut out, print, or paste photographs that embody the trumps as you recognize them. I recommend avoiding reality TV, tempting as it may be, because we know they're not reflecting purely incidental moments. Producers guide characters into storylines that occur inorganically. I recommend aiming for organic experiences. Also note that the news, television news in particular, and cable news even more than that, isn't all that far off from reality television. It is, in fact, competing for the same audiences. Television news will focus on the most violent, negative aspects of any story. Make sure that if you're using these as sources, you're attempting to find a balance—and aiming for the purest embodiment of the trumps.

Debrief: This particular activity never really needs to end. The formality of taking pictures will wake you up to the world around you, but once you've gone through all 22 trumps, you will likely find it hard to *not* see them everywhere. This is a good thing. For a while, I was watching a lot of YouTube videos of landscape-painting tutorials. This was a way of relaxing, born out of my childhood love of Bob Ross. I have no particular artistic ability and never wound up using what I'd learned—but having watched so many, I suddenly found myself constantly aware of the play of color and light around me. Driving down the highway, I began imagining how I might achieve certain layers of color. This isn't all that different from the experience of buying a new car, and suddenly seeing everyone around you driving the same brand. Once we make something a habit, we become hyper aware. As a tarot reader, this is the best possible outcome. Better yet, some of those mental snapshots you take will inevitably appear to you as you read the cards. That picture of the pregnant woman calming her child in the park with the scraped knee will suddenly come to you when reading the Empress, and you'll have an understanding of the card as a real-life experience you never would have had without doing this exercise.

We *could* stop here. This activity takes us deep into the world of the trumps in ways many of us never really go. But we're not going to! Let's think a bit more about what archetypes are, and how we can work with them. The dictionary definition of the term is simply, *a typical example of a thing; a symbol or theme in art or literature.*

In tarot, I tend to think of the archetypes as visual metaphors. In a sense, visual rhymes that depict a feeling or experience in life. They represent something but aren't actually the thing. The give us a way of accessing the thing, remembering the thing, but they aren't actually the thing.

There's a wonderful documentary about Joseph Campbell called *The Hero's Journey: A Biographical Portrait.* In it, he describes a contrary-minded radio interviewer who wanted to sound smarter than the great subject of his interview. The interviewer tells Campbell that a metaphor is just a lie. Campbell manages to tease out that the host has actually no idea what a metaphor is, and he scores a great academic point. It's amusing. But Campbell also gives us a useful definition of what a metaphor is. He asks the host to give him an example of a metaphor. The host says something like, "she runs like the wind." Campbell explains that such a statement isn't a metaphor; it's a simile. "She is *like* the wind" means she's similar to the wind. The metaphor is that "she *is* the wind."

Clearly nobody *is* the wind, but in calling this nameless "her" the wind, we understand something about this woman that goes beyond "she runs fast." We understand her to be wild, uncontrollable, uninhibited, natural, powerful, mercurial, and capable of being both lovely and cooling, as well as intensely destructive. We have a picture of woman far more colorful and useful than someone who can win a race.

Nothing in the trumps are literal representations of anything. Death/13 is the greatest example, since writers have gone out of their way in modern times to distance trump 13 from a prediction of physical death. Even Waite, in *Pictorial Key*, describes this key as a "mystical" rather than physical death. And Waite doesn't shy away from the shadow aspects of anything.

We go to such pains in modern tarot to explain that Death isn't actually a prediction of *dying* because we have a stranger and more distant relationship to death than did previous generations. We're further away from it—many of us, in fact, feel we can escape it if we try hard enough. We don't have a way of accessing it from a place other than fear. As I've said time and again, the world has changed dramatically since the divination tools that are popular today were created. Even the coffin of Lenormand is interpreted today as "ending," rather than physical death. I support this. I don't need a deck of cards to tell me I'm going to die. I've spent more sleepless nights meditating on that fact than I'd care to count. But because death can feel so far away to so many of us, thanks in part to the development of science and medicine, we devote a great deal of attention to explaining how this card isn't literal.

We shouldn't need to expend that much energy, though. *Nothing* in the trumps depicts anything remotely literal! Look through them. If the Empress comes up in a reading, do we express to the client that they're due to become the monarch of a foreign land? If the Moon appears, do we say that the client's lot in life is space exploration? No. From the Hanged Man to the Tower to the World, we're exploring life through metaphors of the human experience. Only Justice and Temperance come close to having any literal relationship to modern life—but when we see Justice in a reading, how often is it engaging on legal battles? Rarely, if ever—especially since many of us rightly refuse to read for legal issues for fear of getting sued. Every trump is a visual metaphor, an archetype, for something we experience. At no point does the Devil appear in a reading and indicate satanic experience.

The trick of course is to connect 16th and 17th century archetypes to life as we know it, today. You've already begun that in the activity above, but let's take it further in yet another activity.

Activity 7.2: In My Life

Objective: Explore each archetype of the trumps in terms of modern life. *Why you should do this:* It's another way of grounding the metaphors of tarot trumps into the experiences that we're reading about for our modern-day clients.

Instructions:
1. Using the table below, consider each trump listed to the left. In the column labeled "people," make a list of people you know or types of people you've encountered who embody that trump. In the column labeled "experience," list experiences from your life that the

trump itself embodies. In both cases, list as many as you can think of.

2. Take a break.
3. Look critically at each of the examples you noted. Does each truly embody the trump, or does each trump embody the experience? Be sure you feel strongly that the connection is real and memorable. Strike out or re-assign anything that doesn't quite fit.

TRUMP CARD	PEOPLE	EXPERIENCE
THE FOOL		
THE MAGIGIAN		
THE PAPESS		
THE EMPRESS		
THE EMPEROR		
THE POPE		
THE LOVER		
THE CHARIOT		
JUSTICE		
THE HERMIT		
THE WHEEL		

STRENGTH		
THE HANGED MAN		
13		
TEMPERANCE		
THE DEVIL		
THE TOWER		
THE STAR		
THE MOON		
THE SUN		
JUDGMENT		
THE WORLD		

Debrief: This list isn't meant to create an exhaustive definition of each of the trumps. In fact, because the trumps are so "big" — they literally trump the other cards in the deck — there should be a fluidity to their meanings that goes beyond that which we explored for the pips. If we're truly listening to the cards, they will tell us unexpected things. Still, unless we're using one of the modern decks that shows people in modern dress and situations on the trumps, we're working with archetypes born from 17th century Italian nobility. By actively connecting those images to modern people and experiences, we unlock those "arcana" and demand that they make themselves useful in our lives.

Earlier we talked about how the tarot follows the rules we set for it. The trumps can frequently flout the rules, especially since we give them so much power over us. We are told by the esotericists that they embody the lost knowledge of ancient wisdom; that they represent the paths on the Tree of Life, and create the ladder used to reach true spiritual enlightenment; that these represent the biggest, most dramatic parts of our spiritual lives, and that they are the single most important part of the tarot deck. How could such big ideas consent to any rules that little old we may be brave enough to impose on them? *Because they're just cards.* And if, as a reader, I have a vague relationship to them, they will control me and remain as evasive as the High Priestess and her mysterious scroll (from the Waite-Smith deck). By doing what we're doing in this chapter, we are gently—but firmly—setting rules that the trumps will be bound by. Like the pips, the trumps understand that they're there in service of the reading. But if we don't set the rules, they'll set them for us.

Again, I say this purely through my own lens and as a result of my own experience as a reader and a client. There are many folks for whom the trumps are clear as glass, and don't require these kinds of activities. Allow me to say this, though: as a client, many readings I've been given have had such a high tone and impractical voice, that I've found them just vague enough to be entirely frustrating. I have limited patience for mystical answers about practical things. When I ask about my job, I don't want an answer that explores my spiritual journey. I want to know how to make more money. That's it. That's all. Far too many readings I've had have gone a little something like this:

CLIENT: I want to know how I can improve my chances of getting a promotion.

READER: Ah yes. I'll draw a card to explore what you can do to get that promotion.

(*Reader shuffles and draws the Magician.*)

READER: The Magician! This is a great card. He tells us to channel the energy above and bring it to fruition below. All these tools on the table demonstrate that he has the skill to do it.

CLIENT: OK.

READER: That'll be 35 dollars.

CLIENT: Hold up. What's that actually mean?

READER: You don't know what 35 dollars means?

CLIENT: I know what *that* means. I want to know what it means to "channel the energy above and bring it to fruition below."

READER: It means that there's all this juicy energy above you, up in your spiritual path, and you need to channel that into something productive.

CLIENT: How do I do that?

READER: You use all these tools.

CLIENT: What tools?

READER: The ones on the table.

CLIENT: How do I do that?

READER: You already have the ability within you.

CLIENT: Yeah, but I'm telling you that I don't know what tools we're talking about and how to use them.

READER: Look within yourself.

CLIENT: I'm doing that, and I don't see anything.

READER: But the Magician indicates that you can, if you look hard enough.

CLIENT: I'm looking hard, and I don't see anything.

READER: You're clearly not looking hard enough, then.

CLIENT: Look, I just want to know what actual thing I can do to get this job I want.

READER: Channel your energy toward it.

CLIENT: *How do I do that? –And if you say "use the tools in front of you," I will set this place on fire!*

READER: I'm calling security.

CLIENT: CALL THEM! YOU NEVER ANSWERED MY QUESTION!

READER: YES, I DID. THE MAGICIAN TOLD YOU WHAT TO DO! NOW GIVE ME MY 35 DOLLARS, BECAUSE I DON'T GIVE REFUNDS AND I DON'T MAKE EXCEPTIONS!

J.W. Ocker, a great travel writer who blogs about his experience visiting creepy locations worldwide, wrote a wonderful book called *A Season with the Witch.* In it, this Halloween-obsessed husband and father moves his family to Salem, Massachusetts, for the month of October to experience the season in the "Witch City." He visits several tarot readers and has a miserable experience with each one. Each provides him a series of vague platitudes that don't relate to anything, and leave him feeling had.

I don't believe for a second it's because the readers are bad. In fact,

I think this stems in part from his hope that these readers will tell him something surprising without providing them any sense of what he wants a reading about. I've already discussed my feeling on general readings.

But I also think the readers share a little of the blame. We too easily settle for the mystical when the practical is desired. More than that, we don't do a good enough job advocating for clients. For example, only in the last year have I noticed—peripherally—that when people ask for readings, they frequently don't know what they're supposed to "do." That begins with asking a question. Many people approach a reading with a sense of curiosity, but once we start working together, they don't know where to begin. They don't know what to ask, or they don't even know they should ask something at all. I used to think, "That's strange—they're the one who wanted the reading." But it's not remotely strange, and it's taken me 17 years to realize that. Unless they're coming to the table with experience as a reader, themselves, why *would* they know? Of *course* they don't. And I could sit there and silently judge, or I could advocate for them right out of the gate. From the second they request a reading, I could explain the experience as simply as possible, explain what they will get from me based on the kind of question they ask, and then help them come up with a question that suits their needs. Being a good reader is about being a good client advocate. In the customer service world, we frequently talk about how "customers don't get training." What we mean is that the customer experience should be intuitive, because, unlike people who work for the company, we don't tell them how to use our website, for example. We have to be good customer advocates.

Once we get into the reading, we need to remain a good customer advocate. We need to answer the question as clearly as possible and be as useful as we can be. The sample reading above is partly tongue-in-cheek, but it reflects readings that I've had as a client. And, with full account-ability, it reflects readings I've given. There was a time in my reading life where, if the client didn't get what I was trying to tell them, I assumed it was the client's fault. Worse, there were times where I got frustrated that the client would *dare* ask about his love life, when we had all the myster-ies of human experience to explore with these magical cards! How could he not be *above all that?*

The reality is that most people who want readings are in a state of desire or crisis or both. They want something they can't figure out how to get, or they're in a pain they want release from. They're far less con-cerned about their spiritual path than we might be. And that's OK. And that's not to say nobody ever is interested in the more spiritual or psy-chological, but in my experience people generally want to know about the practical.

We each may have started our tarot journey in order to explore our own spiritual path, and that is clearly valuable. We can't foist what we want on others, though. If we're reading for others, we need to address what they're asking us, and we need to avoid the temptation to become a latter-day A.E. Waite. Waite may have helped give us tarot, but it didn't come easy. He has made us earn it with his inscrutable style and intense air.

Even if our advertised approach is a spiritual one, we should check in with the customer to make sure that what we're saying makes sense to them. The jargon we've developed as readers won't be familiar to muggles.

Think, for example, about working with the know-it-all I.T. person in your office, or talking to a particularly careless healthcare provider. You approach your I.T. person with a problem, and they "solve" it by showering you with an array of words and phrases meant to demonstrate their clear and deep knowledge of their chosen career. But it makes zero sense to you. You want to know how to get your e-mail to stop crashing, and the I.T. person is going on about processors and gigabits and whatnot, and you just want to do your job! You want an I.T. advocate when your e-mail is crashing. You want to be taken care of. You want to know what you're being asked to do as clearly as possible, so that you can actually do it. And more than anything else, you don't want the obvious answer: "Did you restart?" How many of us in life have been asked by a tech support person if we restarted our computer before calling them? It's the most devastating response in the world. Don't give your client the equivalent of, "did you restart?" And don't give them the equivalent of a lengthy dissertation on alchemical properties at work in the Magician. Even if the Magician in this reading is all about alchemical properties, talk to your client like a human rather than an adept. We have to make sure that it makes sense. We have to make sure that the analogies we're using are clear to the client, that when they walk away they know what we said.

"As above, so below," may make sense to the reader; but if the client cannot parse that phrase, the reading has failed. Help them understand, without talking to them like they're morons, that the Magician means relaxing into the work, rather than putting pressure on the muscle. Help them see that they're suffering from performance anxiety, but if they can release that and surrender to the experience, they will feel their confidence and their skill explode. And if that language doesn't make sense, try again. Ask questions. Compare the experience of the card to experiences in real life. That's why we're doing what we've done above—connecting the trumps to people and experiences we've had in life. So that we can use those when talking to clients. And, frankly, when we're talking to ourselves. Because there have been countless times where I've laid out the cards, seen the Magician and thought, "Oh, yeah, be a conduit!" Then swept the cards up and moved on without pushing myself to give myself a helpful answer. Without taking that idea of being a conduit and exploring how I might actually *do that in real life.*

When we're faced with the trumps in a reading about something practical, we have to give more than the esoteric. Even when the reading is about something larger, we have to make it make sense. If it's an advice reading, tell the client *specifically and practically* how in *real life* he uses those tools, what those tools are, and what to do with them. And if you don't know, work with the client to understand.

Let's look at how that reading *should* have gone:

CLIENT: I want to know how I can improve my chances of getting a promotion.
READER: Ah yes. I'll draw a card to explore what you can do to get that promotion.
(*Reader shuffles and draws the Magician.*)
READER: The Magician! This is a great card. He tells us to channel the energy above and bring it to fruition below. All these tools on the table

demonstrate that he has the skill to do it.

CLIENT: OK.

READER: What tools do you have in front of you that make you a particularly good choice for this job?

CLIENT: I'm not sure....

READER: What are your special skills?

CLIENT: I never really think about what my skills are.

READER: OK. What about this job draws you so much?

CLIENT: Well, aside from the pay increase, I've already been doing it most of the last two years. Nobody really notices, but they've been handing me this work because they didn't have anyone else to do it. Now this job opened up, and I have to apply and go through the whole process, and when I asked my boss about it, he said, "Oh, I didn't even think about you for this. Yeah, throw your name in."

READER: Great.

CLIENT: I know.

READER: So, your boss didn't even realize that you're doing the work already.

CLIENT: No, it's infuriating.

READER: It really is. And you basically have the skills for the job, because you've been doing it.

CLIENT: Nobody sees it, but yeah. I've been doing the processing, I've been working with the stakeholders. I've been putting together the project plans and actually building the budgets all along. I mean, frankly, I feel like I should just get the job by default, but it's opened up to everybody—inside and outside the company.

READER: OK, so what I hear is that you've already got the skills, you're already doing it, but your boss isn't seeing it and has taken it for granted for a couple years.

CLIENT: Basically.

READER: So, let's think about the Magician, right? I said at the beginning that he's got all these tools on the table in front of him, and he can channel that into something good.

CLIENT: Yeah?

READER: Look how they're laid out on front of him, like that. They're totally visible; they're totally exposed.

CLIENT: It looks like he's doing a magic trick.

READER: It does, and he's a magician, so this may involve some sleight of hand, right? Like you probably can't walk into your boss's office and say, "Hey, idiot. I've been doing this damn job for two years! What the hell?"

CLIENT: Yeah, that won't go over well.

READER: So, what the Magician, this magic trick, is showing us is that we somehow need to make your boss see how you have these skills. If you make a big deal about it, if you are too obvious, it'll look like you're calling him out. But if you can creatively find ways of laying out all your tools on the table in a way that makes your boss feel like he's discovering this talent in you, that will likely give you an advantage over other people who might apply.

CLIENT: How do I do that?

READER: Good question. What are your thoughts?

CLIENT: I don't really know.

READER: How does your boss like to get information?

CLIENT: He's totally data driven.

READER: Do you save all the stats about your work?

CLIENT: I haven't, but they're easy to find. What if I gather all that stuff and put it together in my portfolio and my cover letter?

READER: That's a good idea.

CLIENT: I can compare what things looked like before I started doing all these things to after.

READER: I like it.

CLIENT: Yeah. I'm not super good at selling myself, but this seems like a good way to do it.

READER: Right, because you're not being arrogant; you're showing the results of what you've done, and at the same time demonstrating you've got the chops to do it.

CLIENT: So, if I do this, I'll get the job?

READER: Well, we have to think about the question we asked—which was, "How can I improve my chances of getting this promotion?" That's what this card is answering. We can look at whether or not you'll get it in another reading, but it's worth keeping in mind that interviews can be hard to predict, because there's so many moving parts. We don't, for example, know what kind of people will apply and how many there will be. But we can try to see where things are headed.

It's easy to dismiss this scenario as something I made up. You could say I wrote it out and it went the way I wanted it to. And yet, I gave the client a pretty passive personality. He doesn't know what he's good at, he feels like he's being passed over, and he doesn't really feel fully engaged in actually *doing* anything. The reader, on the other hand, keeps asking questions. The key isn't any particular gift beyond being thoughtful about how the card applies to the context of the question. We didn't get the reader's inner monologue, but if we had, it might have started out something like this: *OK, I know the Magician uses his tools to get what he wants. How does that apply to this reading? I have someone who wants a job. What tools would we be talking about? Interviews are about measuring skills. So, we're talking about what skills he has. So, let's start by figuring out what the tools are that are laid out in front of him.*

This happens quickly—more quickly with frequent practice. And, of course, it's easier in written readings, because we don't have to improvise. But the dialogue above involved a lot of the reader trying to make sense of the card in the context of the question—and she managed to do it without expressing doubt or getting wound up in esotericism. She also managed to redirect when the client made an inference that wasn't part of the equation. The client jumped to the conclusion that doing this will get him the job. The reader wasn't afraid to point to the original question. She also managed to initiate a conversation about her ethical views on prediction in this case, so that she was clear about what she feels is possible. But she didn't do or say anything to make the client feel like he was stupid for having asked it.

With that in mind, let's get some more practice with making clear, precise, and practical connections between the big ideas of the trumps and the kinds of questions we get asked.

Activity 7.3: Connect the Dots

Objective: Make clear, modern, practical connections between a trump card and a banal question.

Why you should do this: It's a good way to strip away the mystical in favor of the kinds of answers clients want in times of desire or crisis.

Note: This doesn't mean erasing from your memory any mystical meanings that you use and enjoy. We're adding to the database, not subtracting.

Instructions:
1. In the table below, look at the trump card and the question asked of it. Give the imaginary client a meaning for the card that is practical, precise, and free of anything vague.
2. If you have people in your life who are supportive of your tarot practice, ask them to look at your list of answers and tell you how clear (or not) your response is.
   a. You may want to ask your friend to consider the following questions as they review your answers:
      i. Does this make sense?
      ii. Is this something you could put into practice in real life?
      iii. Is there any jargon or terms in this reading that you don't understand? If so, what and why?

      iv. How would you feel if I read for you and gave you this answer?

b. If you do get feedback from a friend or peer, review their answers. If anything was unclear, vague, or too full of jargon, work on revising for clarity.

c. Note that if you don't have close friends nearby who support this work, there are now countless groups on social media filled with people who are willing to work with peers on this kind of thing. Reach out to them. You'll be surprised. Just make sure you read the rules of the group to avoid violating them. Moderators can be uptight about rule breakers—especially where the group is part of a revenue-generating membership for a larger organization.

TRUMP CARD	QUESTION	ANSWER
MAGICIAN	Where should I go on vacation, this year?	
13	What's the best way to make my co-worker like me?	
THE SUN	I don't know why I'm feeling so exhausted.	

HANGED MAN	I don't want to go to this thing with my husband, but he really wants me to.	
HERMIT	Why are my kids so cranky this week?	
THE MOON	How is my date going to go, tonight?	
FOOL	I want to do something fun on my cruise. What should I check out?	
THE WHEEL	What's the best way to get my boss's attention?	
EMPEROR	How do I make my son clean his room?	
THE LOVER	What's the best way for me to meet the man of my dreams?	

Debrief: As I've said and will say again and again, my aim isn't for you to do away with whatever spiritual connection you have with the cards. The Empress can be a totem of nature, earth's bounty, fertility, the Goddess, and spiritual fecundity. It can also say, "Look, there are people out there who think you can't do this, and you actually can—so go do it."

How did I get that that from the Empress? Because female rulers of countries historically were last choices, given the throne thanks to a king's inability to produce a male heir. Their councils were all men, many, if not all, of those men thought they were by nature of their sex better suited to the woman born to the job. Yet, as the new saying goes, she persisted. Think of Queen Elizabeth I. Thus, when the Empress appears, sure, there may be something to be said about bounty and fertility and Goddess energy. But when it comes to solving a problem at work, or in a collaborative relationship, getting my butt in gear and doing the thing nobody thinks I'm capable of is more helpful.

Many of the books on tarot that I encountered in my early days amounted to an exercise in memorization. Mary K. Greer's *Tarot for Yourself* was, at the time, the notable exception. And I studied dutifully and learned my definitions. It involved many years and even more books, notes, and journals that I would keep and lose, moments of feeling stuck while reading for others, and a feeling of shame when I needed to reference either a book or my notes for an answer.

When we approach the cards by working through our own lens, memorization is almost entirely unnecessary. When you have a moment of understanding the Empress as a woman who shows them all how it's done, despite everyone's doubt, that's harder to forget than it ever is to remember.

The other thing that helps is forcing ourselves to find meaning in the cards even when it feels next to impossible. Because there are times when that happens. And when that happens, doubt creeps in. And when doubt creeps in, we start reaching for anything that sounds good. And that's when we race to the easy answers and to the vague. When we accept that *somewhere* in the cards that were pulled is a practical answer to a practical question, when we demand of ourselves a helpful answer, we grow.

Hence, the following activity:

Activity 7.4: Practical Practice

Objective: Make practical connections between the trump cards and banal questions.

Why you should do this: To show yourself that it can be done, but also to find practical information in the most esoteric of cards.

Instructions:
1. Read each question in the table below and consider it in the context of the question being asked.
2. Create as practical and "real life" an answer as possible. Don't worry about the "right" answer. Give a *helpful* answer. Being right isn't the issue, here; being practical is.
3. Take a break—a day or more.
4. Come back and look at your answers. Can they be more practical? Again, not can they be more "correct," but can they be clearer and

more helpful? If so, give it another try.

Question	Card	Your answer
Example: Where are my keys?	*The Magician*	*On a table with a lot of junk on it.* How I got there: Frankly, just by looking at the picture. Sometimes the most logical answer is the right one. I could go into detail about sacred space, etc., but looking at a Marseille Batteleur, what I see is a table with a lot of stuff. I think about my table at home, similarly riddled with junk. That's frequently a place where I lose my keys, because I can't see them among the detritus. This begs the question, "Do I really think one can locate missing keys with tarot cards?" Honestly, I don't know that I'm capable of such feats—that seems to suggest a kind of psychic skill I don't know that I possess. That said, I guarantee there are folks who can. And if I could achieve that level of specificity in my readings, I'd quit my day job and go on the road slinging cards everywhere I could.
How do I break my writer's block?	The Moon	
Where should I go on vacation?	13 (*La Mort*)	
What's the reason I can't sleep?	The Sun	
Why can't I stop thinking about Albert?	The Papess	

How do I resolve this argument with Kate?	The Empress	
What if I quit my job and started a New Age shop?	Judgment	
Why am I still single?	The Hanged Man	
If I go back to school, will I be able to get a promotion?	The Fool	
My husband and I have fallen into a rut. How can we spice things up?	The Tower	
What will be the result of my litigation against Gary?	The Lovers	
My son wants to join the army. Should I let him?	The Emperor	
Where's the best place to celebrate our anniversary?	The Devil	
I need to get out of this cycle of self-abuse. Where do I start?	The Hermit	
Everyone around me seems to have more fun than I do. What's the secret?	The Wheel	
I feel like I'm spinning my wheels at work. What am I doing wrong?	The Star	

The guy at work has been flirting with me, but he never asks me out. What should I do?	Strength	
I feel this constant sense of anxiety, and my friends keep telling me to "think positive!" Is that going to work?	Justice	
The school year ends next week, and I'm not sure what to do because I need to declare a major, pronto.	The Chariot	
My neighbor will not stop making a crazy amount of noise, and my landlord says that during the day there's nothing he can do about it. I'm going crazy. How do I stop it?	Temperance	
Everything feels like it's going in the right direction, but I'm waiting for the other shoe do drop. When's everything going to go wrong?	The World	
I don't love my husband. I'm not sure I ever did. How do I get out of this?	The Pope	

Debrief: How'd you do? This isn't easy, but it's also sometimes not as hard as we make it out to be. One of the great difficulties of reading is knowing when we're overthinking things, and when we're simply being thoughtful.

You may come back to this list in a few weeks and find that you have a completely different idea about how the card answers the question. In such cases, it's easy to beat ourselves up for not having gotten it "right" the first time. "I should have known better!" It's a phrase I've uttered before mentally flagellating myself for my ineptitude, many, many times in the days after a reading.

But the sane part of me says, "Nonsense!"

Yoav Ben-Dov, in *Tarot: The Open Reading*, reminds us that nothing that happens during a reading is accidental. If that's so, then the interpretation you came up with during the reading was *the right interpretation for that reading at that time.* Yes, in the days ahead, a more brilliant, clearer, more "correct" interpretation may occur to you. Write it down in your notebook or save it on your iPhone. But don't beat yourself up for not having gotten that idea sooner. You had the idea during the reading that was right for that reading at that time.

With all that said, I'm now going to do something I haven't really done throughout these pages. I'm going to share my answers for the entire activity you just completed—but, and here's the kicker, I'm not going to tell you how I got there. I want you to spend some time thinking about how I did. But I also want you to understand that this is just an activity, a way of exploring these cards. My answers aren't "right" and yours aren't "wrong" if they don't match (or vice versa). My answers are mine and yours are yours, and thank God, because wouldn't it be sucky if the world only needed one of us to read cards?

Activity 7.5: How I Got There

Objective: Explore how another reader interpreted the same card and question combinations you did.

Why you should do this: It can help develop your analytical eye. It's sometimes just fun. It's also worth nothing that this is the only optional activity in the book, but I couldn't stop myself from including it—both so you could see that I've done the work, too, but also to see if you could work backward. Figure out the math from the question and the answer.

Instructions: Look at my answers to the same card combos and questions you answered, and try to figure out how I got where I did. (Note, since I already explained the first one, it's not included below.)

Question	Card	My Answer
How do I break my writer's block?	The Moon	Dig into the darkest parts of yourself, the things you're most scared to let people see, the things you're most embarrassed of, and use that as inspiration.
Where should I go on vacation?	13 (*La Mort*)	One of those places where they show you how life used to be—like where they re-enact old farm life in the early days of the country.
What's the reason I can't sleep?	The Sun	There's too much light in your room.

Why can't I stop thinking about Albert?	The Papess	He makes you feel unique, like something he's never seen before.
How do I resolve this argument with Kate?	The Empress	You have to find a way to convince her that what you want to do was her idea. Diplomacy. If you can covertly exert your power, she'll come around. But you may have to accept that you won't get credit for it.
What if I quit my job and started a New Age shop?	Judgment	People may talk about you behind your back, but it could wake you the hell up.
Why am I still single?	The Hanged Man	Because you're constantly playing martyr, and that tends to be a turn off.
If I go back to school, will I be able to get a promotion?	The Fool	Probably not. You've developed a reputation as a space-shot, and people will have a hard time thinking of you differently.
My husband and I have fallen into a rut. How can we spice things up?	The Tower	Play rough.
What will be the result of my litigation against Gary?	The Lovers	You'll have to choose between your relationship with Gary and the settlement you want.
My son wants to join the army. Should I let him?	The Emperor	Assuming he's fully aware of what that means, it could provide him the kind of structure and development he needs.
Where's the best place to celebrate our anniversary?	The Devil	Spicy food followed by a a visit to a sex club.
I need to get out of this cycle of self-abuse. Where do I start?	The Hermit	Alone. Learn to be alone, and you'll figure out more than you ever imagined.

Everyone around me seems to have more fun than I do. What's the secret?	The Wheel	They're OK letting go, giving in, and not being in control.
I feel like I'm spinning my wheels at work. What am I doing wrong?	The Star	You're idealizing your job. Your romantic point of view is keeping you from seeing things as they are and doing the actual work that gets you ahead.
The guy at work has been flirting with me, but he never asks me out. What should I do?	Strength	Take the reins. He's clearly into dominant women.
I feel this constant sense of anxiety, and my friends keep telling me to "think positive!" Is that going to work?	Justice	No. Cut through their crap. They need to see what you're *really* going through, not what they think you're going through.
The school year ends next week, and I'm not sure what to do because I need to declare a major, pronto.	The Chariot	You've got to make a decision one way or another, or you'll get pulled in all directions and you won't have a real sense of what you're even doing there. How do you bring all the things you're studying into one major?
My neighbor will not stop making a crazy amount of noise, and my landlord says that during the day there's nothing he can do about it. I'm going crazy. How do I stop it?	Temperance	You may need to bargain with him. One hand washes the other. What can you give him that will make him happy?

Everything feels like it's going in the right direction, but I'm waiting for the other shoe to drop. When's everything going to go wrong?	The World	Cut it out. Just enjoy the damn ride.
I don't love my husband. I'm not sure I ever did. How do I get out of this?	The Pope	If you want out, there's only one way—you have go through the system.

Debrief: Allow me to re-iterate that this isn't an answer key; it's simply a peek into my interpretations. If I were to face these combinations on a different day, in another mood, with more life experience behind me, I might answer differently. I would likely answer differently were I reading face-to-face or in a video than if I were typing my answer. The reason I asked you to figure out how I got there was mostly academic—something we rarely do in tarot—figure out how someone else reached the conclusion they did.

Now is the time we start putting the cards into combinations. As mentioned earlier, there are French traditions in which only the trumps are read. Because I'm in the "more is more" camp, I've never really focused on majors-only readings. I like using the full deck, and out of seventy-eight cards, finding I've pulled a spread only of majors. But majors-only readings are popular *and* certainly can provide a great deal of information. And because the trumps *have* acquired the spiritual patina I mentioned earlier, trumps-only readings could be great for readings on that theme, or examinations of large life events.

Again, my mission in focusing on down-to-earth definitions of the cards doesn't mean I think one should never use spiritual meanings. Just because I focus on Marseille-style decks doesn't mean I think they should be used exclusively. Simply that the scope of this particular lesson involves these.

Activity 7.6: Multiple Majors

Objective: Combine several trump cards into one answer.

Why you should do this: It's easy to see each of the trumps as individual archetypes. Because they're so large, it can be difficult to see collections of them as *one* archetype. But if you're answering one questions with three trumps, this can help you get there.

Instructions:
1. Keep the trumps separated from the rest of the pack.
2. Shuffle the trumps and draw three cards to answer each of the questions.
3. Keep your answers as practical as you can, and try to use the three cards to create one answer.

Note: I've included some more spiritual questions, in the expectation that you may need that thirst quenched a bit after all my harping on practicality. Enjoy.

Example: Money has been tight, lately, and I can't seem to put my finger on why. I need to save for necessities, but I'm not managing to do that.

Question: What am I doing wrong?

Cards drawn: The Moon, the Devil, the Hermit.

Answer: You're flat out addicted to impulse and sensual pleasure. You need to practice discipline; you need an ascetic lifestyle, at least for a while.

(Take a moment to figure out how I got there, if you'd like.)[1]

1. What's the best thing for me to do about my son's relationship with these guys who are terrible influences on him?

Cards drawn:

Answer:

---

1   Note that the order of the cards didn't mean a whole lot to me, here. The Devil, which represents both addiction and sensuality is in the middle, and gets a lot of the attention. I didn't focus much on the Moon, although it also suggests sensual pleasures in the form of animal instinct. In my initial thinking, I was going to talk about instinct and animal stuff, but when I wrote out my final answer, the combo of the Moon and the Devil seemed to reinforce each other, and I just wrote about that. I was tempted to talk about how the Hermit suggests the client already knows this and already knows how to get out of it—but I've gotten answers like that from readers before, and I find it frustrating. If I knew, I wouldn't have asked. So I had to force myself to think in terms of an actual step—and the Hermit to me suggests discipline and giving up on the sensual pleasures.

2. There's something missing in my spiritual practice. I need something, but I don't know what. Where can I start to relight that spark?
Cards drawn:
Answer:

3. The dog keeps getting out of the back yard. How do I keep him there?
Cards drawn:
Answer:

4. Marriage is not as easy or as sexy as I imagined. Is it always going to be this difficult?

Cards drawn:

Answer:

5. I can't stand my new boss, but I can't just get a new job for various reasons. How do I make this better?

Cards drawn:

Answer:

6. I've been desperately in love with Erin for three years, and she's not interested. How do I get over this?

Cards drawn:

Answer:

7. I'm pretty sure my wife is cheating on me. What do I do?

Cards drawn:

Answer:

8. He's gay, and I'm not. I know how he feels about me, and I don't have any problem with it—I just don't have the ability to feel anything more than friendship. I know he's suffering, and I want him to feel better. How do I help?

Cards drawn:

Answer:

9. I watch the news and feel constant anxiety. I know I need to stay informed, but I also know I need to stay sane. How do I balance that?

Cards drawn:

Answer:

Debrief: In writing this activity, I thought about using the same format as the previous one—in which I gave you the question and the three cards. I use that technique so that we have a common language, and I can show you what I might have done. Where I show examples in this book, it's partly to set you up or debrief the activity as though we were sitting together; it's also partly to give you feedback, at least in terms of whether or not you're on the same page I am from a style perspective. This time I elected not to do that, because, by this time, you're likely itching to get your hands on the cards. And because the time has come to start giving yourself feedback. So rather than debriefing this lessons with the same kind of summaries throughout, you should end this lesson on the trumps by debriefing yourself. You are by now as expert in these techniques as I am, if not more. Put on your expert hat.

Use the space below to describe what you've learned so far. What has helped? What hasn't? What will you use and what will you reject?

Interlude 4:
◊   ◊
On Being Wrong

I go back and forth about whether or not a reading can be wrong. Camelia Elias, who it's clear I admire, suggests that, no, the reading isn't wrong. If the querent can't understand the answer, or he thinks it's wrong, that's because he's not willing to hear the message he needs to hear.

There's a part of me that agrees. Christine Jette, in her marvelous book *Professional Tarot*, discusses how readers need to be aware of the myths clients tell themselves. They don't do this because they're bad; they do it because it's a survival mechanism. We all do it. We tell ourselves certain things about ourselves as a way of handling the world. An extreme example, I suppose, are those people who have suppressed horrible memories from childhood. In order to get through life, they need those things to *not* have happened, otherwise they wouldn't be able to get out of bed in the morning. When the mind/body finally "allows" them to remember, it's for a reason. Less extreme examples include the daily myths—she doesn't like me because she hates men, he doesn't want to go out with me because he can't see what's good for him, my boss doesn't understand how hard I work.

The reality is that tarot readings can frequently give us answers we don't particularly want to hear, or that we aren't ready to hear. If a reading cuts to the quick, if it tells us something that disrupts the mythology we've developed as a coping mechanism, we can immediately discount it as wrong. This is another mind/body protection mechanism. We aren't ready to hear what the cards are telling us, so we discredit the reading as "wrong."

When clients tell us we're wrong, it's possible that we're right, but simply that we've struck a vein they can't yet explore. And, unless we know the client incredibly well, it's unlikely we'll have any true sense of whether or not that's the case.

On the other hand, I'm a human, and as such I've got biases and my own myths about myself. While I try not to project my own wants and needs onto the cards, there are times where that's inevitable. We all do. Someone, for example, who was hurt deeply because of an infidelity, may see infidelity everywhere in the cards. Or nowhere, as it's possible they may be working overtime to protect others from suffering a similar pain.

My mother told me when I was young that a tarot reader predicted the death of her father. I don't know what the reading was like and what was said; I wasn't born when my grandfather died. But I do know that my mother is incredibly resistant to tarot and tries to actively avoid anything I post on Instagram that relates to it. It doesn't matter that I've told her I don't have the ability to predict that kind of thing. She was wounded by that reading, the result scared her, and it doesn't matter what I say. She *knows* what she *knows.*

We all have our biases, as they're deeply ingrained. And because they're based largely on what has hurt or scared us in life, they are difficult to break down.

If the client is flawed in that way, it's pretentious to assume I'm not. And so, yes, I do think there are times when I'm wrong. But, again, I can't know for sure. And when I'm "right," as we've discussed, when the client gushes over how on the money my reading was, I can't know if it's simply because I've validated the myths they tell themselves.

This is all by way of getting to the central point: don't worry about being right. This isn't school. You're not taking a test. None of the activities we've done together are being scored, and because they're all fake readings, anyway, who cares? But beyond that, own what you see. If you agree to do a reading for someone who asks where their lost keys are, and the Magician tells you that they're on a table full of stuff, and it turns out that they're on the passenger seat of the car? Oh, well. You've learned that you're not the kind of reader who can find lost keys. I'm probably not, either. Welcome to the club. "But what," you wonder, "if that person thinks that I'm bad at this???" To which I say, "Oh, well."

There are those folks who want to test our "powers." To see if we're any "good." I say, go ahead and try. If that's what you want out of a reading, you're going to be disappointed no matter what I say. You're not interested in whatever answer I might give; you're interested in how right or wrong I am—and, as I have said before, *this isn't a test.* There isn't a right or wrong in this game. And it is a game. And if someone is coming to you to figure out right and wrong, they have larger issues than can be solved by a tarot reading.

There are, ultimately, few decisions in life that are irrecoverable, and the ones that are shouldn't be handled with tarot readings. "Should I take my own life?" No tarot! Therapy! Doctor! Please! "Should I keep the baby?" No tarot! Counseling! The other stuff, the stuff we generally read about, isn't life or death. "Should I quit my job?" Yes or no, that question generally won't directly lead to death or dismemberment. Unless your job provides health insurance, and you know you've got an illness that could kill you. In which case, no, don't quit your job; you need insurance! You don't need tarot cards to tell you that! "Should I quit my job?" Can you feed your kids? Yes? Do it or not. No? Wait until you know you can feed your kids! Do you see where I'm going? Life or death stuff doesn't belong in readings, and everything else—I mean, who cares? You quit your job to start a band, the band never takes off, you get another job. Will it be harder to get another job because of the three years you weren't working? Maybe. But if you talk about how you were self-employed and the lessons you learned during that time, you may impress the hell out of an interviewer, and maybe you'll get a job you never thought you'd get.

Starting a reading with the pressure to be right is pure perfectionism. One of my favorite writers, Anne Lamott, says in her wonderful book *Bird by Bird: Some Instructions on Writing and Life,* "Perfectionism is the voice of the oppressor, the enemy of the people. It will keep you cramped and insane your whole life....I think perfectionism is based on the obsessive belief that if you run carefully enough, hitting each stepping-stone just right, you won't have to die. The truth is that you will die anyway and that a lot of people who aren't even looking at their feet are going to do a whole lot better than you, and have a lot more fun while they're doing it." She's right in every possible way. You don't have to be right, you don't have to be perfect, and your readings will feel a lot better if you let the blood flow through your body, instead of constricting it with the desperate need to impress. You're not giving readings to be impressive, you're giving readings because you're an empathetic soul who wants to help people. Help them, and if they say you're wrong, well, they can go to hell! I mean not literally, but who cares if your friend thinks you're not good at tarot? They still love you. And if they don't, then they literally can go to hell.

I've spent a lot of my life in the theatre, and there are times when I look at what's playing on Broadway—or even in regional theatres—and I think: *People like that? That guy can't write! That lady can't sing! Why are people lining up to see this shit?*

Because there's no accounting for taste, including mine, and so why spend our lives trying to be impressive, when at the end of the day, people are going to turn on the TV and watch *Desperate Housewives of Westchester County* whether we like it or not?

Here's the truth, as harsh as it seems: *Some people will not like your reading style.* OK? There will be people who think you're bad at this.

Here's the rest of the truth: *Other people will like your reading style.* OK? And why let the jerks who don't like your reading style take up all the space in your head? Sure, maybe they're not actually jerks just because they don't connect with your work, but the people who like what you do? They're the ones you're reading for. Maybe there's not as many of them as you'd like, but wanting more people to think you're talented is ego. And ego isn't the same thing as success. Success is getting what you do in front of people who want and appreciate it. Ego is wanting to be famous and loved by everyone. There is nobody who loves everybody. The person in tarot, or whatever field you enjoy, that you most love, that you most admire, the person who you think most embodies your ideal will be hated by someone else. Because, and I include us both in this, *there is no accounting for taste.*

Moral of the story: Give yourself permission to just do this, and give yourself permission to let go of the need to be "correct." Give yourself permission to see someone else's interpretation of the cards, and think "OK, well, that's what *they* think." Taking a break, just now, I scrolled through Instagram to find an interpretation of the Devil that made me think, *that's not what that means!* It's what it means to *that reader.* Give yourself permission to be you. Right or wrong.

PART III:
THE VISUAL
LANGUAGE OF
TAROT

The Visual
◊ ◊
Language of Tarot

Tarot is a visual medium, like it or not. And there are times I don't like it, because I'm not the most visual thinker. One of the reasons why I fell in love with Marseille-style decks is that the absence of scenes on the pips felt suddenly like I was liberated from something I didn't even know I'd been constrained by. Again, allow me to say that this is not a criticism of situational pips. Most of the decks in my collection are situational, and I've backed at least four such decks on Kickstarter in the last few weeks. But there was a moment of looking at the pips and suddenly feeling naked in the best possible way.

But tarot is a visual medium, situational pips or not. And since we have not yet even considered what the cards look like, the time has come to do that. Because whether you're similar to me and aren't by nature the most visual thinker, or you see vivid images wherever you go, this is another tool you want in your tarot toolkit. And even in the simplest of pip decks, there are worlds of information available to us based on what the cards show us—even when they're showing us nothing more than eight coins in two neat rows.

Lesson 8:

Visual Language

Suppose a client asks me, "Should I take this new job?" And I draw these cards:

Looking only at the images, what would you say the answer is? Note it here.

My answer: "Hell no!"

How did I get there? I see three, increasingly big X's! I immediately thought of the American gameshow, *Family Feud.* Each incorrect answer earns a big old X and a buzzer to go with it. If I look at the meanings of the cards, I get coming together, stability and foundation, and beauty. But if I'm looking at the images, I see X's saying "STAY AWAY!" And that's what we're talking about.

Did you get a different answer? Did you say "yes"? *For shame!*

I'm joking, obviously. The point is not that we have the same answer, but that you have a reason for saying so. If this had been the same numbers in the suit of swords—that notoriously negative and painful suit—I would have said "yes." Why? Because I would see essentially three openings.

"Come on in, the water's fine," those pool-like shapes would say to me. And, as such, I would urge my client to run, not walk, to this new opportunity. If I got odd-numbered swords in the Marseille tarot, I might say, "this opportunity isn't actually open to you anymore." Why? Because I have openings with swords blocking an entrance.

What of the cups or coins? What about a combo of different suits, which is far more likely than what I've chosen in this example? That's for later in the chapter. Calm yourself. This was purely to show us that such things are possible.

Throughout these examples, I will be using specifically the Marseille

Tarot—so that we're all looking at the same thing. But note that these techniques are adaptable to all decks—including Waite-Smith decks. If you strip away all your preconceptions about what's happening in the picture, and look fuzzy-eyed at them merely as shapes in context to other shapes, you will come to surprising insights and fresh interpretations, I guarantee.

Let us, for the time being, return to the trumps. Since, in Marseille-style decks, they are the most visually active, this will be a good way to start. For the purpose of these activities, I'll be using images from one deck, so that we're all on the same page. But because I know you're hungry to get your hands on whatever cards you've got in your collection, I wholeheartedly recommend repeating these activities again with whatever deck you'd like—including any Waite-Smith that strikes your fancy.

Directionality plays a huge part. I'll share my thoughts with you for one example, then we'll get into a similar activity. Let's consider these three cards:

What do I see out of the gate? The Hermit to me seems to have right of way, so to speak. He is the deciding force. He's between two fairly dramatic images, but he's turning toward one and away from the other.[1] Out

....

[1]   The Hermit frequently faces left, but it depends on the deck. That's why I sug-

of the gate, my instinct suggests there is a choice being made—away from destruction, and toward awakening. Because I'm reading without a question, never my favorite thing to do, I'm forced to figure out what this suggests generally. But, working purely from the images, I see a bright (the lantern) man of a certain age (the Hermit) turning to something that resurrects (all those people in Judgment) something. He's deciding against (turning his back) something that can be destructive (the Tower).

As I go more deeply, I see that there are people who have been in this destructive tower and have been harmed by it. For some reason, given that the Hermit is traditionally a learned person, I'm getting the sense that the Tower suggests academia. I frequently hear people in academia refer to it as the "ivory tower," and it can be incredibly insular. Towers are insular—I'm thinking here of a traditional association with the tower in Lenormand decks.[2] So my guess is that this is a person who has given a lot of life to academia—or something similar—and has found it to be incredibly harmful to him. It's already hurt several people close to him. He's turning back to that, and looking toward—what? The past? In many readings, the left represents the past and right represents the future. But I don't get that sense here. In fact, the idea of Judgment as awakening— these people coming from the grave—seems to be that he's waking up to *life.* As in *real life.* As in the world outside the golden tower of academia. This tells me that he's leaving behind this harmful world of academia and taking his lessons out into the real world, to share what he's learned

gest using my images first—so that we're on the same page—and then repeating with your own cards.

2   I recognize that tarot and Lenormand are *different systems* and *never the twain shall meet*, especially in terms of meaning. But if you haven't gotten by now that the rules make me cranky, well, then I just don't know what to say to you anymore.

with the "real people" (a phrase that makes me anxious, because who is and isn't "real"? But for the sake of this reading I'll go with it). Here's an incredibly smart person who is leaving universities behind to go and do workshops or speaking engagements with audiences who want to hear what he has to say. Here, too, is someone who is going back to life—in the sense that he's going to be part of the "real world" once more, and who may discover that the theories he's been working on for all those years in the tower of academia have real-life consequences. Or that his learnings will be altered once he comes into contact with the world as people are living it, and not the world people theorize about from inside the fortress of college life.

What I say to this client depends a lot on the context. This is a general reading, but in general readings people sometimes indicate things they want to know. They'll express a need for advice—even if they don't say what they need advice about. Or, they'll express a need for insight into a situation. They'll also, if you're paying close attention, provide clues that may help you Sherlock Holmes some context. For example, suppose this client said to us, "I just want a general reading right now, because work isn't good." I know that they're probably looking for some kind of validation about work being bad, and that maybe they're not sure how to get out of the situation. In which case, I might frame my interpretation of these cards: *It looks bad, it looks like work has had a destructive impact on some folks you're close to, and you're realizing it may hurt you, too. It seems like you're looking toward some awakened folks who might help you. You're clearly smart and experienced. What do you think this is suggesting?*

If they're sitting with me, I can ask that question. If not, I may just say what I think—which I described above. *It's probably time to wake up to the possibility of exploring life outside of this institution, where you'll be engaged with people who are open to what you have to offer.*

If the client said to me, "What do I do about work?" I'd say, *Get out. It's destructive. There's a path that involves going out among the people and waking up to the world outside of your job. But if you stay, you're going to wind up like the folks who've stayed and gotten hurt.*

If the client said to me, "I want a general reading about my love life," well, I'd have started from a completely different point of view. In that case the narrative I sussed out earlier makes no sense, and I have to think differently. In this case, the Tower looks like a sexual object or organ. The Hermit is walking away from it, and toward judgment. I might say something like, *The purely physical relationships you've been involved in haven't gone well, and might have left one or both of you hurt. You've come around to the reality that some time alone might be wise, but at the same time you can't stop thinking about the physical. The physical isn't bad, but it needs balance.*

Why do I say he can't stop thinking about the physical? He's trying to stay on the straight-and-narrow, but he's holding his light up to see all those naked people. There might even be an element of sex addiction, here; though that crosses slightly into a medical field I'm not sure I'm qualified to get into. I might ask whether they have ever found themselves thinking about sex to the point of distraction, and whether they might want to explore counseling for that. Again, though, in a general reading, it's tough to say. I could draw more cards, and if I saw an excess of wands, I might say there was definitely some sexual obsession going on. Wands are, after all, as phallic as can be. Swords, to my mind, aren't particularly phallic, although one does thrust with them. In the Marseille decks, there's definitely something vaginal in their arrangement. And the odd numbers, as we already discussed, are crossed with a single sword. A host of these arrangements would suggest to me certainly, if not an obsession, an imbalance. Cups and coins would be a tempering element, in this case—at least visually. And remember, we're talking about the images, right now.

Reading in this way is a two-step cycle. The first step is to discover a narrative from the images; the second step is to check the narrative against the question. The stronger or clearer the question, the easier it is to check the narrative against it. I called it a cycle rather than a process, because you are constantly shifting back and forth between steps. You develop an initial narrative, check it against the question, refine if necessary and then further the narrative, check it again, refine, and so on, until you have a sense of the answer.

This is not the method I reach for primarily, but it has become immeasurably helpful—particularly when a reading is full of trumps. In a spread of three cards, where I know the three will work together, *a la* Robert M. Place's method, to answer a single question, the cards don't have set spread positions. As we explored earlier, we need to look at the narrative of those cards and parse it—not unlike parsing, or diagramming, the grammar of a sentence. In three cards, I'm looking for the subject (who), the verb (action), and who or what is acted upon and how (the direct object or the adverbs/adjective). In the example we walked through just now, I figured out immediately that the Hermit was the subject. He was in the middle, he was the most active human figure, and he was, in a sense, walking toward something. Somehow the Tower became kind of a noun and a verb, because I realized immediately that the Tower was his job, and that the job was destroying him—but destroy is the important part. I've never interpreted the Tower that way, to be honest, but the combination of the Hermit—a wise man—with the cliché of academia as the Ivory Tower made me think it was about work. He was moving toward something—so in a sense, he is also a subject and verb—in this case, Judgment. Judgment looks like people waking up, hearing the call. In my head, the Hermit becomes the angel in Judgment, as he works with a more democratic population of people who *want* to hear (they're awake to) his message.

When I interpreted that from the love life point of view, the context changed and so did the grammar. The Tower became sex, probably purely physical and really rough sex; the Hermit moves away from it. Here the Tower is the subject and the Hermit is the verb—because the Hermit represents moving away. And he's moving toward awakening. That's the general definition of Judgment, but I can't help but see him looking at all those nudies! It's possible he's awakening to a healthier view of the human body as more than a series of sexual organs, but it's also possible that, despite his wisdom, he can't shake his more puerile tendencies. He reminds me of the guy who goes away to a retreat because he needs to learn about himself, and winds up sleeping with as many people as he can during the weekend. He's not ready to be alone with himself, because he can't completely exist outside of sex. That's what makes me think about sex addiction as a possibility. But since I don't have a degree in psychology, and I'm not in the business of mental diagnostics, I avoid that language and focus on the more general aspects.

If this person were sitting in front of me, I would need to be thoughtful about checking my narrative. I have an active imagination, and we already talked about bias. I know people like this Hermit I'm describing. I need to check my narrative against what my client has told me to make sure that I'm not imposing my own life onto his. Still, everything I found in that narrative came purely from the images on the card—and, as such, I do need to trust it. Would I have concocted this narrative out of thin air? No. But with the cards before me, it's what that visual language is telling me.

Because tarot *is* a visual language, grammar seems like one way of making sense of it. But I don't want you to get any more turned off by it than you did with my math analogies, earlier. You don't need to have an advanced degree in English to do what we're talking about. You don't need to remember what gerunds are and whether or not you can split an infinitive.[3] What you need to do is look for the card that seems like the active one, the card that seems like the main character, and the card or cards that describe. That's about it. From that, you craft your story and check it against the question and what you know about the client.

And, as always, this takes practice. Which is what we'll do right now.

---

3   You can, by the way. Screw pedants who say you can't.

Activity 8.1: Check Yourself

Objective: Answer client questions using three trump cards and the visual language of the images.

Why you should do this: It will help you practice using the visual language primarily, and also allow you to think about checking your narrative against the question and what you know about the client.

Instructions:
1. Read each question and client profile, below. The question is what the client asked you, and the profile is what you happen to know about them—either because they're friends, or they've told you.
2. Pull three trump cards for each question and use the techniques we've described to come up with an answer. You can use your definition of the trump as support, but the primary interpretation—the narrative—should come from what you're seeing in the cards. (You don't need to use my subject, verb, object approach, but it can help.)
3. As you work through your narrative, check it against the question and the profile to ensure you're coming up with something that fits the context of the reading.
4. Finalize your interpretation and create a concise answer to the question, based on your narrative.
5. Take breaks, throughout, as you need them.

Question	Profile	Cards drawn	Your answer
What's the best I can hope for in this friendship?	You've known this client for years, and while he likes people in theory, once he gets close to them you've noticed he nitpicks everything until he talks himself out of pursuing relationships.		
I'm not sure what I should do next. There's potential for a promotion, but I'm not sure if I should go for it.	Elsewhere in the conversation, this client mentioned she's had this job for ten years and never imagined staying in it. It was a summer job in college, and she got promoted twice.		
I think my girlfriend is cheating on me. What should I do about it?	She casually mentioned earlier that she thinks a co-worker is out to get her, and that her last few relationships have fizzled because of trust issues.		
I'm wondering whether Carrie has any interest in me, or if she's just being nice.	In the small talk before you began reading, you learned that the client, Dan, is already in a long-term marriage and Carrie is happy with her partner.		

I'm feeling incredibly stuck at the moment. Nothing is working the way I want it to, and all the potential options I see wind up being dead ends. I don't know how to get out of this phase.	Having read for this person several times, you've been asked the same question several times. When you make suggestions, the response is frequently something like, "I don't know if that will work." As a result, you've detected finally that this person has a problem with defeatism.		

Debrief: Later in this course we'll talk more about narrative, but in this case you probably used the "story" of the cards interplaying with one another to create a narrative. You've also created a narrative that includes what you know about your client. Sometimes you don't know much; sometimes you know a lot. But if you're paying attention, you can usually catch a few cues that will go a long way into helping you refine and finesse your reading.

When debunking fortune tellers, cynics frequently say that the teller is reading the client more than whatever divination tool they use. I remember an episode of *Designing Women* in which the famously logical Julia demonstrated how easy it was to bilk unsuspecting clients by simply watching body language.

What seems incredibly illogical to me is that anyone thinks being able to read people *isn't* part of the reading. When reading for someone, I'm not watching their eyes to see if they narrow when I ask a purposefully vague open-ended question. But if they're sitting in front of me, their body language can tell me whether or not they're nervous, skeptical, open, closed, interested, or bored. What they say about things other than the question they're asking can clue me in to what they really want to know. The kind of question they ask can clue me in to the things that they're thinking about. That isn't an act of conning anyone; it's an act of awareness, that makes the process of reading easier.

The visual language of tarot isn't just what the cards say. It's what the client is saying to you, if they're sitting in front of you. If they're not, that makes it harder—but based on what they tell you, and how engaged in the process they are, I have a sense of how the reading will go.

Someone once bought a reading from me as a gift for a friend. I e-mailed the friend twice over three or four months before I got a response, and a third time alerting them that I would be unable to read for a six-week travel period. The friend promised me that she would have a question for me soon, but it wasn't until I was already on the road that she finally sent it to me. It doesn't take a personality expert to get that this person didn't have much interest in a reading. And when I uploaded the video and sent her the link, to this day I can see that she hasn't watched it. Several months later, the reading is likely to be both inaccurate and irrelevant. (The cynic in me thinks, "I wonder when I'll get an e-mail telling me how useless and wrong the reading was.")

Everything communicates, from the images on the cards to the way the client is sitting. And the more we can gather from what we see, the more layers we can add to the reading.

Having explored the trumps and their visual interplay, let's look at the pips again. To keep us consistent, I'm using the same Marseille-inspired tarot deck for these initial examples. But in the practice activities, you can use whatever deck you'd like. I would recommend a deck that has some variation in decoration from pip to pip. There are pip decks that simply repeat the pattern without any adornment, and that's fine for reading—but in the case of the visual language, you'll want something that has some variation.

Let's look at the Two of Swords, the Four of Coins, and the Five of Cups, pictured below. Examining the images on the cards, rather than the meanings we've developed for them, we can see a few things:

- The floral pattern (known as an *arabesque*) on the Two of Swords is larger and more ornate on the inside of the oval; outside, it is simple and small.
- The two crossed swords create a womb-like space within, and an unguarded space without.
- All four of the coins are separated and enclosed from the others because of the branches.

- Similarly, the branches of the arabesques on the Five of Cups separate the bottom set of the cups from each other and the top, and the two top ones are separated from each other.
- The branches on the Four of Coins and Five of Cups seem to be going outward, expanding, there's a push outward.
- There's an overall sense of privacy, or a sense of in and out in these cards—what's on the inside, what's on the out, and what's kept apart from the others.

Note that, where I've qualified something with words like "unguarded," "protected," or "inward," this is simply my response to what I'm seeing. I have no evidence that the artwork is indeed outward-growing, or meant to imply embrace. All I know is what I see.

Were I forced to read these three cards without any sense of what the individual cards mean, I could come up with something interesting. And that's as someone who doesn't necessarily have a visual mind. But even as I began describing the flow of the branches or flowers, I noticed a few themes: There is a great deal of isolation and separation (all the objects separated within the card, including those within the oval of the swords. The most dramatic "growth," the flowers on the Two of Swords, are the ones most protected and isolated. The tiniest, also on the Two of Swords, are the most exposed.

Given only that, I might suggest that this reading is about someone who feels safest when closed off from others. They feel incredibly vulnerable in public or social settings and prefer isolation wherever possible. In fact, they thrive most in isolation. That's a pretty classic introvert trait.

But I also see that while there is a safety in that, there's a central desire to branch out (all those out-going branches). The impulse to expand outward is there—though it's not the strongest energy, it is the central energy. So, I see a reading about a person who is incredibly isolated, and likes it that way, but wants in a small way to branch out.

This isn't necessarily a great reading in terms of answering a question. But remember, there wasn't one. However, if my client had asked me for a general reading, I feel confident that I've painted a picture that might give her insight about her life. In fact, I I might have made more sense from a general point of view then if I had worked with the elemental and numerological combinations of the cards.

That said, combining the situation I described based on the decorations with the more common numerological/elemental meanings allows me to take three cards and go even deeper. Thus: The Two of Swords gives me a feeling of growing awareness, the Four of Coins gives me a sense of financial stability, and the Five of Cups gives me an emotional upheaval. So now I see a picture of a person who feels more creative and productive when they're isolated, but they're starting to realize that their financial stability may be tenuous if they don't go out into the world (remember coins as duty), and that's causing emotional turmoil. But I know in the center is this seed of willingness—those outgoing branches—at the center of the reading. So all is not lost. Like any seed, it needs care and watering to grow. But the cards show me it is growing (that feeling of expansion I got), so it's not like we're starting from zero. This person clearly has the potential to do it; they're just going to have to make a commitment to it, and wrestle with that feeling of safety they so crave.

Remember how I said I dislike general readings? I do, but using the visual language of the cards to provide a foundation helped me answer a question the client may not have known she had. Now, if I were reading this, I would wonder: *What happens if the client says she's not isolated, doesn't have any financial issues, and doesn't feel emotional turmoil?* Well, in that case, I'd be wrong. Which means I should probably give up reading, accept the tarot as a fraud, and go back to passively wondering what life has in store for me. I could also try two alternatives to throwing in the towel: dig deeper in what they actually want a reading about and re-contextualize my initial impulses; or, look at that Two of Swords and its protected vegetation and understand that I've hit a nerve that wasn't ready to be hit.

Yes, there's a part of me that feels as though that's an arrogant response. But on the other hand, a client telling me I'm wrong doesn't necessarily mean they're telling me the truth.

One of the things that gets in the way of adults learning new things—old dogs learning new tricks, as it were—is ego. If we feel like we stand to embarrass ourselves, or we're going to look like fools, it is less likely that we will take the risks required to learn. Sadly, in order to learn anything we don't already know how to do, we have to start from square one and that means we're going to look like novices. Quick example: Whenever I visit New York City and I take the subway, I can immediately tell who the newest residents are. Not through intuition. I know it because they are the people on the subway most loudly proclaiming how well they manage to navigate the subway system, and describing in detail the combo of trains they'll take to get wherever they're going. I never hear people

who've lived in the city for any appreciable time bragging about their subway prowess. It is, to me, the surest sign of a newbie.

I'm not making fun of those new New Yorkers. I've been that person in
various points in my life. Not living in the city, but in places where I wanted to appear more expert than I am. I did when I started reading tarot,
and I see it with people who are new to reading. Because the adult ego is
so fragile, we're constantly aware of trying to show how much we know,
so that it's clear to others that we deserve a seat at the table. But that's
problematic, because if we're busy trying to prove our prowess, we're not
actually learning anything new. For years, when I was still acting, I would
use every acting class I took, not as a learning opportunity, but as a desperate chance to prove to others how good I was. When I think back on
all the money I spent doing that, I could kick myself. Not just because I
missed out on some great lessons, but also because nobody cared how
good I was. That's not why anyone was there.

This may feel like a digression, but it's not. Life isn't much different
than the New York Subway, learning tarot, or taking an acting class: We
are all, at many times in our lives, newbies in our way. We are all at times
in situations where we are not expert, and in which we have no idea what
to do. And when I tell my client that this is a time when there's a slow
awakening that financial stability means going out into the cold, cruel
world, and she tells me that's false, it may in fact be because I've made
her feel like the newbie who needs to show off how well-versed she is on
the A train.

I can't ever know for sure whether I'm right or wrong. I could second
guess myself after every reading—and there are times when I do—but

then I'd never do anything. I see what I see, and if you can't or don't see it, then, maybe we're not meant to be reader and client. And it's taken me a long time to get to that point. And it's not just with people I don't know. I'm frequently most nervous reading for people that I know, because their impression actually means more to me. If I read for a friend, and they hate what I've done, then I'm far more likely to feel devastated by it. But my friends are no different than anyone else, in terms of their ability to see what they don't want to see (so am I), and whether they think I'm a good reader or not has no bearing on whether or not we love each other. It's just ego. And if I let my ego get in the way of friendship? Well, I've got bigger problems than my talent at divination.

With all that said, let's try one more example together. Then, you'll get some practice on your own.

Randomly drawing from my deck, let's look at the Ace of Wands, the Four of Wands, and the Six of Coins.

Before you read my description, take a moment and explore your own impressions. Remember, too, that this isn't in order to compare yourself to what I eventually tell you, but so that you can practice coming up with your own version. That's the version that matters to you. Mine is just a way of showing you how I got where I did.

What I see:

- Ace of Wands: A powerful club bursting out of nowhere. It's raining seeds, or flames. It is strongly a "masculine" image, but the hand has a tight grip on it.
- Four of Wands: A firework. This outward reaching explosion of light and color, expanding in the sky, brilliant and beautiful, but brief.
- Six of Wands: Two triangles—like huts—made of coins, with two chimneys of smoke coming out of each one. They're a mirror image of the others. There's also a square, within, like the body of a house, with a central door-like floral decoration.

These impressions I wrote even more quickly than before. And I allowed myself to get a bit more fanciful. That does seem to be what the reading wanted of me, though, judging by how I was feeling about the Ace of Wands as I saw it first. There's kind of a supernatural element to this reading, which I hadn't expected. But the first card set the tone for me, and I went with it. Again, if you saw other things—and I would be stunned if you hadn't—that's good. This is what I saw.

Now my job is to take this and make it into a reading. Unlike the first example, I don't see themes quite as easily—other than the idea of bursting forth. The Ace of Wands has a bursting quality, and so did the Four of Wands. As I'm looking at what I see and describe, my instinct begins to paint a picture of someone who is bursting to get out of the house. I saw all those house-like images in the pattern of the Six of Coins—but even with my idea of the two chimneys, I get a sense of energy—steam—trying to get out of a restricted environment. So even if the home isn't a literal one (with coins it could also be work), there is a need, an impulse, an anxious urgency to burst out and burn the whole place down! There's a real locomotive power that wants to come forth. I see someone, probably young (I start with an ace, and that certainly ain't old), desperate to get out of the nest—to get out from somebody's tight grip.

When I add the meaning of the cards as I understand them, I do get support for that. Certainly the Ace of Wands has a bursting out of the nest quality. There's a fire and passion to go forth and *do*. To be somewhat coarse, this card has a quality of ejaculation to it. It's a phallic image, with sperm-like drops falling around it—a desire to go out and sow ones oats. The Four of Wands suggests a stable passion here, which I take to mean "sustained passion"—as in this burst to go forth has been going on for a long time. It is a foundation of their being. And the Six of Coins, which is beauty (six) and/or double growth (three and three) in life (coins), suggests a desire to expand one's horizons. So in this case, the visual language of the cards combined with the meanings that I have developed for them essentially confirms my thesis. That's a nice thing.

Camelia Elias talks about finding evidence in the reading. I've taken this as a cue in my reading. I look for an initial thesis, and then attempt to prove that thesis with research—the other cards in that spread. If the other cards don't support my initial thesis, then I either revisit the thesis, or I attempt to explore why there is a differential. Mostly, I follow my gut as to how to proceed. Sometimes the reading not supporting the thesis can simply be because the thesis is change, or because life or the client's actions are undermining that impulse. Sometimes it means that my initial thesis was underdeveloped, and I can go back and re-assess.[4] Either way, it's a helpful way to consider and test one's own readings.

Activity 8.2: Picture those pips!

Objective: Create answers for client readings, using only the visual language of whatever deck of cards you're using.

Why you should do this: As we've seen, reading this way can create an excellent foundation for a general reading. It's also a good tool to reach for when the usual meanings of the cards aren't connecting.

Instructions: Pull three pip cards for each for the questions below, and use only the visual aspects of the card to come up with a meaningful answer.

1. I just want a general reading.
2. I'm not sure what to do about Randy at work. He keeps looking at me. I know it's not a harassment thing, but it still makes me uncomfortable.
3. I am desperate to get out of this relationship, but we've just moved in together—and he left his job for me. I don't even know how to get out of this. I know I should have said something sooner, but I didn't realize until he was here that I am desperately unhappy.
4. My boss keeps taking credit for my work. I can't come out and tell

---

4   This is yet another reason I'm so fond of written readings.

him to stop, but I need him to see what he's doing. How do I broach that topic?

5. Dating apps have absolutely failed for me, and I'm just not a club kind of person. How do I get out there and meet people?

Debrief: For those who are used to more pictorial pips, or like me, don't particularly think in images, this can be challenging. I'm not really capable of doing it myself, unless I take the steps I did in the examples above: namely, free-associate in sort of a bulleted list what I'm seeing, and then work out the meaning of those images. That said, it's good practice to do it, and it's a skill that can add a tremendous amount to a reading.

Activity 8.3, Part 2 (Optional): Use the meanings of the cards to expand and add color to the reading examples you performed above.

For the first time in all these pages, let's put the entire deck together. We will combine the pips and the trumps and use only the visual language to create meaning.

Let's do an example together:

King of Wands, Ten of Swords, the Fool

Again, take a moment before reading my work to do your own. It's better to do yours first, otherwise it's easy to get contaminated by my thoughts.

What I see:

- The King of Wands is looking at the swords, and the Fool is looking off. Everyone is looking to the right, so toward "the future."
- The King is posed to rise, as though he's using his wand as a cane. He also has a somewhat prissy posture, that suggests something of an attitude.
- The King is looking vaguely at the interweaving at the top of the swords, but he doesn't appear particularly focused on or interested in them.
- The swords create kind of a thick, impenetrable encasement—but they also pierce that opening—so they're breaking their own security, so to speak.
- The Fool isn't paying attention to any of this, he has no interest, and so walks on.

Themes:
- Forward motion, not looking back
- An attitude of carelessness or thoughtlessness. Maybe disinterest, or even arrogance?

- A self-sabotaging security breach? Like leaving secure information slightly visible (those swords piercing their own center), and the Fool being foolish.
- There's a little narrative of a king's distraction, preventing him from seeing the real danger (those piercing swords again), and as such he loses a lot and becomes a beggar—who hasn't learned anything, because he's still equally, if not more, distracted.

So in this case, I have the rather strange and not-very-flattering description of a somewhat arrogant person who is distracted from what really matters, and doesn't notice how something he thinks is secure is being breached. That causes him to look like a fool. Since the swords represent communication, I would wager that I have someone who is high up in a company, who has left a document or communication out because he was distracted by something else, and could stand to look silly—but probably won't learn much from it.

Not something I particularly want to tell a client, and I suppose if I had to I could cloak this in gentler language. On the other hand, the truth sometimes hurts. And that's one of the funny things about general readings, too. We're told never to ask questions we don't want the answers to, but when you don't ask a question, anything is up for grabs. Also, because this person doesn't really stand to learn much from this experience, he may not believe what I say, anyway.

In this case, I don't need to reach much into the meanings of the cards, because in a way I used them: A King of Wands might be a creative director, or something similar—but I already know he's a leader of others (king). I used the swords to talk about communication. This could also suggest intellectual property. For example, it might mean that he's left copyright-protected information vulnerable to hackers. Because it's a ten, it may be something that the company just finished and has been working on for a long time, which ups its value. The Fool is the Fool, and the image and the meaning in this case were so inextricably linked, that I never really needed to take that one further.

Activity 8.3: Everybody into the Pool!

Objective: Use the entire deck to practice visual readings.

Why you should do this: It's expanding on what we're here to do!

Instructions: Use the entire deck to perform three card readings for the following questions. Use only the visual language, as we've done so far. After you've made it through the entire sequence, you may optionally go in and add more layers of information by using the "meanings" you've developed for the cards. As always, I recommend showing your work. In years to come, you may find it useful to see how you arrived at the conclusions you did.

Question	Cards drawn	Your answer
I met this guy online. What are the chances our date is going to go well enough that a relation-ship might form?		
I feel like an outcast at work. People have par-ties and hang around with each other, and I just don't fit in. They invite me, but I feel like it's pity. Am I being sen-sitive, or do I need to get more engaged?		
I want to get a dog, but the kids are not as re-sponsible as I wish they were. They want one, I want one, but I real-ly don't want to be the one doing all the work. Is getting a dog a good idea?		
I want to plan something special for our anniver-sary next month. What could I do to make this unique and special, something he hasn't seen before?		
I keep dreaming about Dale, and I'm not re-motely sure what it means. I haven't seen him in ages. What is this dream is trying to say?		

Debrief: Even if you never read this way, there's something fun about doing it. For those of us who might not be visual thinkers, it's an excellent way to force ourselves into that way of viewing things. Like anything, practice makes, not necessarily perfect, but certainly better. And tarot is a visual medium, so we owe it to ourselves to try it. For those who *are* more visually inclined, this is simply a great deep-dive into something you already love and feel comfortable with. Whether you fall on the more visual spectrum and found the preceding chapters more difficult, or vice versa, going through these kinds of exercises allows us to deepen our practice and discover more access to the cards. This is especially helpful when we feel stuck. It's happened to everyone. We draw the cards and compare them to the question and wonder what the hell they're saying. Having any of these tools in our back pocket may help spark an answer we didn't think we'd find otherwise.

Activity 8.4: Back to Life...

Objective: Take what you've been doing so far, and bring it into real life.

Why you should do this: It's time to do some real readings in this course. *Instructions:* Using the visual language techniques we've talked about, find some volunteers who would like a free reading. Explain to them that you have an experimental technique you're working with, and then perform a reading using this technique and the whole deck of cards. I've already mentioned how much easier readings can be when you have a question to work with, so you may want to make sure folks have at least a theme they would like to explore. Or, you could use the visual language to find a situation, and then use the meanings of the cards you've developed to supplement that with more information. It's up to you. Now that you've gotten this far, and you're reading for real folks, you get to run the show.

Debrief: This is on-going practice, but it's good to jump in and experiment in this way. Read for as many people as you can as often as you can. And if you're comfortable with it, ask them for feedback.

While we're on the topic, let's talk about feedback. Feedback isn't easy. We need it to improve, but to improve we have to first recognize that we have opportunities for improvement. After years of working in the corporate world, especially in corporate training and adult learning, I've discovered that most of the time when people say they want "feedback," what they mean is that they want "validation." The difference? Feedback is an objective overview of what you did well, and what you might have done differently. Validation is telling you how great you are. We all need validation. Without it, we find it difficult to sustain interest in things. We need to know we're doing at least a decent job. But validation doesn't help us improve, because it focuses only on what we're already doing well. If we want to get better, we need to know where we need to improve.

There's a corporate cliché: "All feedback is a gift." In theory, yes. But if it sits unopened, or if it is ignored, the intention may be well-meant, but the gift itself remains useless. We need to give ourselves the gift of being brave enough to listen to feedback when it's offered.

Accepting feedback is brave. Not like running into a fire and saving a kitten, but it is still a brave thing to do. Most people are bad at taking it. A psychological series of events gets triggered when someone says, "Oh, this didn't go the way I thought it would. Maybe you should try this next time." For some people, this shakes the foundation of their own self-worth. For others, it speaks to a lack of civility on the part of the feed-back giver. And in either case, it throws the relationship out of whack, even momentarily, because one person's sense of self has been violated.

Earlier, we talked about how people build myths about themselves, and what can happen when that myth is shattered by a reading. Well, getting feedback is similar. And what's worse: Not only are most people not good at accepting feedback, almost everyone is terrible at giving it. In regards to ego, it's a lose-lose. We're going to be told things we don't want to hear, we're going to disagree with at least some of it, and in all cases we're going to feel shitty about ourselves.

Still, it's worth getting. And to get better at anything, it has to be gone through whether we want to go through it or not.

People will tell you, "don't take it personally." That's easier said than done. You're inevitably going to take it personally; it's about something you've personally done. It's about something you've put your personal time and energy into. It's something you personally want to be good at. You can't help but have a personal response. Whenever I hear people say, "don't take it personally," I'd like to be a fly on the wall the next time they're told they did something less well than they could have.

How you work with feedback is up to you. What has worked for me, as often as anything can work, is that I don't respond to the feedback right away. I listen, I write it down, I thank the person for offering it to me (when I have the sense of self to remember to do that), and then I let it sit for a while. A couple hours, a couple days. When I'm ready, when I don't feel like my entire selfhood is tied too closely to whatever it was I was accepting feedback on, I return to it. I examine it, like an artifact. And I try to understand it: What could have prompted it? What does it really mean? Are there messages hidden within it? Have I heard this before? The idea is to try to tease from it the kernel of gold within it—to find that alleged gift people keep telling us feedback is. It's not unlike sifting wheat or panning for gold. Instead, you're turning over a piece of advice and trying to make sense of it. What can it really tell you?

There are times it won't tell you anything. There are times when you will feel it's wrong. I recommend being skeptical of times you're *convinced* it's wrong, because that may suggest a blind spot. But just because we've gotten feedback doesn't mean that it's right. If something seems completely and totally wrong to me, I try to have the self-confidence to ask others whether or not that feels right to them. If not, I can throw it away; if yes, I know I have to deal with it, somehow.

Most of the time, it will tell you something. And it may tell you something entirely different from what the giver intended. I had a friend years ago who would always give me feedback on things I'd written. I would look at it, and it was as though she'd read someone else's work. Not only was it wrong, it seemed to be completely disconnected from whatever I had sent her. I started to get angry, frankly, and vowed never to send her anything I'd written ever again. But then I looked at the feedback and tried to take it apart. I realized that her feedback *was* wrong—in a way.

She was wrong about the direction I should take with what I'd written. But she wasn't wrong, because what I had written seemed to want to go in that direction! If I wanted it to go my way, I had to go back, further back than where she had identified the problem, and make things clearer and closer to my goal. I never would have figured that out had I not wrestled with the feedback. And I never would have come close had I dismissed it out of hand.

Be brave enough to ask for feedback, and it will pay you back—as long as you're willing to work with it. And if you've gotten this far along in this course, you clearly have a dedication to doing this—so you've got to be ready to get the kind of answers from clients that will help you improve.

As always, here's your chance to record what you've learned and how it takes you closer to your goals. This is the last time I'll mention that. Part of learning is building habit. The time has come for you to continue this technique without my reminders. Do try to remember, though; it's going to help you retain what you're learning, and it will also prove interesting when you come back and review this in years to come.

Interlude 5:
On Being Right

"The most depressing thing that can happen to a prophet is to be proved wrong. The next most distressing thing is to be proved right."

—Aldous Huxley

Throughout, I've been exploring the idea of trusting yourself and the reading. We've talked a bit about what to do when we're stuck, when the cards won't come together. We've stuffed our tarot toolbox with skills for all kinds of situations. I hope it's been helpful.

This morning, though, someone on my Facebook page asked me a question I'd never been asked before, and it positively blew my mind. I'm quoting her here:

Trying to figure out my skill level in Tarot, I found it easy to facilitate people drawing their own meanings from my interpretation of the spread. I do this for a living using psychological assessments. The freakier part is making forecasts and having them come true. While a yes/no question is 50 percent probability, the appropriateness of the card is not. My friend stopped reading when she saw that her mother had died. She was in another country at the time. While there are videos on when you're wrong, none that I found about when you're right and how you deal with the experience.

Stunning thought, no? We ache so desperately to be right...but then what happens when we are? Throughout, I've talked about my feelings on doing third-party readings—an answering the questions I'm asked, regardless of what the outcome might be. Yes, I've talked about empathy and ethics. But what if I do a reading for someone who asks whether his wife his cheating, and I say, "Yes, she is," and I'm right? There are moments when I'm amazed by the accuracy of readings, and there have been moments when I've been freaked out by what I've seen.

Now, it's worth pointing out I've never predicted a death. I can't think of a situation in which I would be able to see something like that, unless I agreed to a reading on a question like, "Will Donna make it through the year?" and I pull trump Thirteen. Well, come on. But I likely wouldn't agree to such a reading. Probably not even for ethical reasons, but because I don't want to be someone who can see that kind of thing.

But death isn't the scariest thing that can happen to us, despite what my mind might tell me at three in the morning. Truman Capote, as the epigram for his last (unfinished) book, chose a quote by Saint Teresa of Avila: "More tears are shed over answered prayers than unanswered ones." And then he went on to prove Saint Teresa right as rain. Stephen Sondheim gave us a whole musical about it, *Into the Woods.* Sometimes the scariest thing we can do is be right about something wished for. Sometimes the scariest thing we can do is be right at all.

So how do you handle such things?

I don't know. Honestly. Which makes it an odd thing for me to write a chapter about. Yet I've chosen to, because I think it is one of the most important things to consider. This will not bother some people. Some people will find themselves impressed with their own skill. And certainly, when we receive validation that our readings are right on the money, it can frequently feel incredibly good. But there are times when it can scare the shit out of us.

One thing I suppose is to remember what we've said before: don't ask anything you don't want an answer to. It's tempting to do it. We can be like teenagers with a Ouija board, freaking ourselves out over what may be something, or may be nothing. It's tempting sometimes to, in the heat of an impulse, ask: "When will I die?" and slam a card down on the table, then sweep it into the back after only a brief glance—or, on the other hand, to *dwell* on it for years.

The other thing I think is to take what we do seriously. If we agree to do a reading on health or cheating or whether or not there's a chance of getting a promotion, we're making an agreement to get an answer to a question. It's easy to be glib. It's easy to become desensitized. It's easy to take for granted that there is power to what we do. And I say that as someone with a largely secular view of the tarot. I don't believe that the cards themselves have any inherent power. The power comes from the agreement we make with ourselves and the cards as we prepare to shuffle them. But there is still power in answering a question. Whether it's a sacred power or not is up to your cosmology.

For me, it's the same power that comes when a friend asks us whether we like their new significant other. There is power in that answer, particularly if the relationship is fresh. Suppose I say, "Yes, I think this is your soulmate!" Like it or not, I've added an incredible amount of pressure to my friend's relationship. Because whether or not they truly are, I've tacitly told them that if it doesn't work out, they've failed at something. And there will be consequences! On the other hand, if we say, "Well, he kind of dresses weird and has a wonky eye, and I don't like the way he laughs," we've pointed out things that our friend will now be hyper aware of—where they may not have noticed any of that before.

There is a degree to which we don't need cards to answer questions. When people come to me with a question about the state of affairs in their love lives, if I get even the barest details, I can tell whether or not things are going to work out. It's not because I'm psychic, it's because I recognize patterns I've seen many times before. Anyone who is alert to the behaviors of others can usually get a sense of whether or not a relationship will last, or whether a person is likely to open up enough during the first few dates to make a connection. And we know now how I feel about patterns. Likewise, if someone comes to me and asks if they're going to get the job—and they were late to meet me and can't make eye contact as I introduce myself, I already have a sense of how their interview might go.

Questions and answers are powerful things—whether the answers come from a reading, or from our own sense of how things are going based on observations. Having the answer can be empowering. It can also be scary. And then there's the consequence of sharing an answer. I've had friends in relationships that ended, who asked me how I *really* felt about their ex. After downloading all my lingering hatred of their former lover, they get back together, and I'm now the idiot who hated my friend's soulmate. Never again. I've learned.

From "What do you want for dinner tonight?" to "Do you think my husband is cheating on me?" we are taking on a certain amount of responsibility if we answer the question. Responsibility can always be scary.

When it comes to making dramatic predictions, well, that's a tougher one. Making the choice to ask that question means facing the answer we get. And it depends to a degree on one's feelings about how things work. If you get the right answer to a predictive question, is that evidence of a psychic gift you didn't know you had? Is it a fluke? Is it something else entirely? Or is it a different kind of gift.

Suppose you're worried about a loved one—a parent, say. Suppose you decide to do a reading about their longevity or their overall health. Suppose you pull a spread that indicates death. (Again, your ability to do this will have, I think, to do with the agreement you make with the cards—what cards or combination signify a physical death?) That's not the answer we want for anyone we love, but having asked the question suggests to me that you have at least a little inkling that something might be wrong. What prompted you to ask such a thing to begin with? Were you playing a game, like the kids with the Ouija board? Or were you concerned, because there are patterns at play that indicate a terminal outcome is possible? If you see the answer you dread, that they are in fact on their way out, how surprised are you? And what might you do with this information? What if knowing this information allows you to reach out and say the things you never said, or that haven't been said in too long? What if it causes you to reach for the phone and ask for someone close by to check on that person, or be there with them in an hour of need?

If you choose to ask a question and read about a terminal illness, it's worth considering your motivations—and it's worth considering what you plan to do with the outcome. As I've said many times, I don't read for health issues. I suppose I could. Anything is possible. But it's not my place, because I don't believe I have the wherewithal to support someone who finds out bad news. I don't have the training to support someone when they discover they have a terminal illness, or that someone they love does. And I do believe that there is a skill in handling such things. But that's me. And if you do it, and you get the dreaded answer, consider how this could be a gift. After all, you asked the question. (If you didn't ask the question, and you somehow divine an answer like that from the cards, you have a skill clearly greater than mine—and that's something you may want to explore in other ways. But also, does it have to do with the cards you pulled, or are you having a moment of connection with someone who matters to you? Because that has been known to happen. From people just "knowing" something terrible has happened to a loved one, to thinking of someone and having the phone ring, we are connected in ways we don't necessarily imagine.)

Something else to consider is the fear of the self-fulfilling prophecy. Does having seen something in a reading, and then discovering it happened, implicate you in the event? Have you somehow forced something to happen because you did a reading about it? If a reader sees in the cards devastation from a storm or the death of a loved one, is the destruction or death caused by having done the reading at all? Likely not. The reading is simply reporting on patterns, and you're interpreting those patterns. Unless the reading predicted the death of a loved one, and you went out and poisoned their soup, the reading isn't likely going to have had any impact on the experience. It's alerting you to a fact, and—annoyingly—the termination of life is as much a fact as Saturday being the weekend.

Self-fulfilling prophecies can happen. But I don't think it can happen in terms of the well-being of others. Where self-fulfilling prophecies are likely to happen are the times when someone asks, "Will this relationship work out?" And the reading says, "It'll be a struggle." The client moves into defeat mode, and sabotages the relationship before anything good can come from it. That is a situation in which the client's actions, based on the reading, affect the outcome of it. Then again, is that truly self-fulfilling? Or did the reading know they would act that way, and predict the outcome based on that? We have no way of knowing.

Being right in a reading can be thrilling and it can be scary. But in the chapter on magic and faith, I talked about the idea of praying. Those of us brought up in a faith where one prays to a deity in the hopes of receiving an answer often struggle in adulthood when we feel that we're being ignored by the deity we're begging for help. Suppose we view the tarot as a way of communicating with a higher power. If that's so, then we're simply getting the answers we asked for, and it's allowing us to become proactive participants (to the degree that's possible) in the course of our own life events. I don't want to predict the ill-heath or demise of anyone's loved ones. Again, I don't feel well-armed to handle such things from a purely psychological point of view. But suppose you were to see that in a reading for yourself or even for a client—who is to say that that isn't an opportunity to appreciate whatever time remains?

In the PBS documentary about Buddhism, the idea of impermanence was explained as a glass. We get a glass, and we love it—then the glass breaks, and we're sad. But if we accept that the glass is already broken when we get it, then every moment we have with it is special. What if tarot reminded us of the broken glass? Might we not then have the opportunity to appreciate it more while we have it? Or at least to take care of it in its slow-motion fall from the table? I think that's probably about as great a gift as we might imagine—particularly if it helps us accept the inevitable breaking of the glass.

Scary as it might be, being right even in cases we don't want to be right can help us accept what we've got to deal with—an appreciate whatever that slowly breaking glass might be.

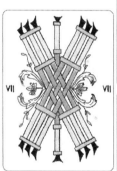

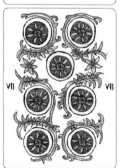

PART IV: PUTTING IT TOGETHER

Lesson 9:

Putting it Together

We've covered an incredible amount of ground together. From numbers and elements, to the feeling the vegetation on pip cards might suggest, we have worked on building and deepening our tarot practice. We've also worked on grounding it—which, to me, is an immensely helpful tool, and a great supplement even to more spiritual tarot practices. After all, it's not just above—it's below, too.

In this lesson, the time has come for us to start putting all we've learned into practice. I have some exercises for you to try, and they'll hopefully be as fun and useful as those that have come before. But, really, the time has come to take it to the streets. At the end of the last lesson, you took the visual language and conducted real reading with willing friends. In essence, reading for others is the place this whole book has been leading to and you've already done it.

NARRATIVE

One of the great skills of tarot readers is creating a narrative. Narrative is one of the basic human needs. Food, water, air, love, and narrative. It's how we make sense of things, and how we report what happened. Great readings frequently, especially for longer spreads, have a decent narrative. But the idea of narrative can be misleading and it can cause unnecessary anxiety. Narrative readings aren't all that difficult to do, and you don't need an MFA in creative writing to bring them into being.

Early in our time together we talked about the "math" of tarot: Element + Number + Context + Question = Meaning. Then, we added the trumps and spreads, and we begin thinking about the "grammar" of tarot. The narrative of readings really takes those two things and puts them together.

With the pips, the Two of Coins might be: *Duality + Duty = Having two equally important jobs to take care of.*

As we added more and more, a question about whether now was a good time to date might be notated, mathematically, as: *Is it time to start dating + duality + duty = you might be able to start dating, but you also have to take care of life at home in equal measure.*

That's already working with narrative. And if we wanted to, we could take it even further with a three-card reading:

(Is it time to start dating) + [(duality + coins) + (seed + passion) + (foundation + feelings)] = You could start dating as long as you recognize that your passions might get away from you at the same time you're feeling more emotionally stable than you are, so make sure you're addressing the

emotional and the practice in equal measure.

A nine-card multiplies all that by three. That's one reason I like working in multiples of three—inspired by the work of Robert M. Place. Because a spread becomes a series of equations of *question +card 1 + card 2 + card three.* If we wanted to get crazily notational, we could document it, thus:

Question + row 1 = theme; [Row 2 (card 1 + card 2 + card 3) + Row 3 (card 1 + card 2 + plus card 3)] + [column 1 (card a + card b + card c) + column 2 (card a + card b + card c) + column 3 (card a + card b + card c)] = validation of theme; validation of theme + theme = answer

Is that insane? A little. But not really. This diagram may make that easier to see.

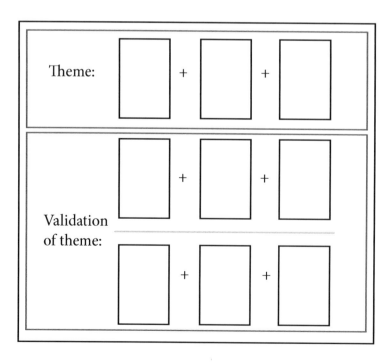

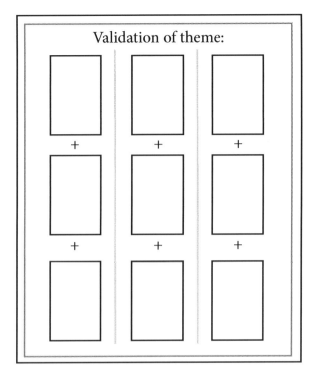

But linking the cards together and creating narrative is nothing more than the math of tarot that we learned earlier. It's adding everything together and coming up with a sum that answers the question asked.

When you're writing a reading, it makes things easier. Even people who don't consider themselves writers manage to create narrative in their writing, because they're so used to reading it. Don't believe me? Go find an e-mail where you described to one of your friends something unusual that happened to you.

But written or aloud, there are simple ways you can strengthen the narrative thread of your readings. Let's look at an example using three cards.

Example 1

Question: I want to buy a new house, but I'm not sure if it's the right thing. What will happen if I make that big purchase?

Cards drawn: Hermit, Ace of Coins, Ten of Wands.

This question lends itself to narrative, because the querent is asking for a story. "What will happen if I..." So right out of the gate, we have a good set up.

There are a couple ways to do this, but let's start with the most straightforward. Let's look at each card in the reading as a "plot point" in a story. Or: first this happens, then this happens, then this happens.

Take a moment and try that out yourself, using these three cards. Note your story below. Then, read my example. Don't cheat. By this point, I trust you to try it yourself before you look at what I've done. Also remember that our comparisons are not about quality; they're about different examples of the same thing.

Your narrative
First this happens:

Then this happens:

Then this happens:

My narrative:
First, you wind up spending a lot of time alone, then you find you don't have much money to spend, then your enthusiasm comes to a close.

Your answer will depend entirely on the relationship you've developed to the cards, by this point. But I'll explain my answer, based on my relationship with them. I'm choosing to read the Hermit quite literally: time alone. Likewise, the Ace of Coins—you literally have just a penny to your name. Finally, I look at wands as "passion" or, in this case, enthusiasm, and ten as the conclusion of that suit—concluding enthusiasm.

My narrative doesn't quite answer the question, but it's a start. I need to craft that narrative into something that will answer the question. I don't need to use my "first draft" as gospel, but I should try to hew at least fairly close to it. If your narrative actually answers the question, you're done. But if not, try it out there. Then read what I've come up with.

Your final answer:

My final answer: You're going to wind up stuck doing this by yourself, and your finances will be severely curtailed. At least in the foreseeable future, your enthusiasm for this purchase will wind up burning out.

If you noticed, I didn't change all that much, but I did phrase it in a way that allowed for a clearer, more specific answer to the question. It's still a narrative, but I used my initial version as the outline, and then drafted a better, clearer version. It says more or less the same thing, but it answers the question better.

Another way to do it is to engage the subject, verb, modifier approach. You can use that as an actual spread (i.e., the first card is subject, second card is verb, third card is the modifier). But I like to let the cards tell me what they are.

Using these same three cards, I'm looking for the most "active" card as the verb—the action. Aces and tens are fairly active, and based on the energy of these cards, I'm not super convinced that one is more active than the other. But the Hermit, though he is "doing" something (walking, holding up a lamp) is incredibly passive, at least as I view the cards. So I'm going to say the Hermit isn't my verb. And I'm going to say that my Ten of Wands is the verb, because wands are super active, and coins a little less so. Fires burn; earth *is.* So, the Ten of Wands is my verb. The subject is the Hermit, and the modifier is the Ace of Coins.

When I say "modifier," grammatically what I'm talking about is the adjective (describes a thing) or adverb (describes an action). That may be triggering memories of terrible English classes where you couldn't re-member the difference between a gerund, an adjective, or an aardvark. So let's simplify by saying that the modifier means the word that says "why" or "how." Our sentence will read this (the subject) does this (the action/ verb) in this way or for this reason (modifier). Whether the modifier is the how or the why will depend on the combo, but for the most part should be pretty easy to detect—it isn't ultimately all that different.

When I use this method, I will frequently reorder the cards in that way, so that I'm reading as such. You don't have to, and moving the cards can feel like a cardinal sin. It's not, though, and I encourage you do to do the things that feel like sins, anyway. At least when it comes to tarot. I mean, according to a lot of churches, the tarot itself is a sin, so why shouldn't we sin a little more?

So here's how I would reorder them: This (the Hermit) does this (Ten of Wands) in this way or for this reason (Ace of Coins). *(See above.)*

Take a moment and create your narrative.

Your narrative:

My narrative: A wise person concludes her passion because her finances are small.

Again, my narrative is a first draft. I need to do a little finessing to answer the question, but as you can see the ultimate answer isn't all that different from my first one. I made this a "wise person," though my first instinct was to call this a "lonely person" (Hermit). I didn't, because I figured that might be insulting. It's presumptuous of me to suggest that someone is lonely. Although I still think that loneliness is a result of buying the house, not that this person is an especially reclusive human. And I can elaborate on that in the final answer. Beyond that, the answer was more or less the same: your finances are diminished and your enthusiasm wanes.

You see how moving the cards using this technique didn't actually affect the answer. This combo, with this question, and this reader, at this moment in time, is likely to come up with the same answer. It's a matter of the method that helps me best come up with a useful narrative that then allows me to best answer the question. Thus, I get:

My final answer: You're wise enough to know that you'll be broke and spending all of your time alone. Your enthusiasm will burn out because your finances are so diminished.

Different words, same meaning. The nice thing about this is that you don't have to feel like choosing one method will stop you getting the "right" answer. Your destination will likely be the same; you're just taking a different route to it. Your GPS will still get you to the same place, because *you* are the variable—not the method you use.

Activity 9.1: Story time

Objective: Create an initial narrative to help answer the question, then a final narrative that answers the question.

Instructions: Draw three cards for each of the following questions. Write an initial draft using one of the methods above, then create a final draft that answers the question.

1. What is the reason my partner and I keep fighting?
   Cards drawn:

    a. Initial narrative:

    b. Final narrative:

2. When will I find my soul mate?
    Cards drawn:

    a. Initial narrative

    b. Final narrative:

3. What happens if I don't end this relationship with Matt?
    Cards drawn:

   a. Initial narrative:

   b. Final narrative:

4. Everyone thinks I'd be perfect for this job, but I don't see myself getting it. Do you think I have a chance if I apply?
Cards drawn:

   a. Initial narrative:

   b. Final narrative:

5. What if I go back to school?
    Cards drawn:

    a. Initial narrative:

    b. Final narrative:

Debrief: You can see that narrative in the case of these readings, at least in this style, isn't so much telling anyone a story. When we hear narrative, it sounds as though one has to begin with "once a upon a time" and end with "happily ever after." Not so. What we're really talking about is an answer to the question told in a way that puts the querent (or whoever the reading is about) into the role of protagonist who does things or to whom things are done. That's about it.

A note on spoken readings: I've extoled the virtues of written readings above, and it's no secret that writing is my predilection. Just because I find them easier to do, doesn't mean they actually are. And my love for written readings comes in part from ego. I don't like clients hearing the messy parts. I want them to see me lay out the cards and seconds later provide them with a cogent answer that blows their minds. Because I can handle all the mess off stage, so to speak, written readings appeal to me. But people prefer face-to-face or video ones, and why shouldn't they? When you're paying for something, you want to see that some effort went into it. The result may actually be less useful, but if you can sense the effort that's gone into it, you feel at least like you got your money's worth. It's an odd thing. It's also a more personal experience, because you're being *talked with.* You know this reading was meant for you. And extroverts in particular like being engaged in that way. Frankly, just because something is easier doesn't mean it's the right way to do it.

In my case, I give clients a choice. I briefly explain the virtues of written (faster for me to respond, quicker answer) and video (more personal, longer, more like face-to-face), and then the downsides. But I let them choose.

Spoken readings are a skill as much as anything else and require practice. There's a tendency when speaking not just to read the cards, but to try to teach the client how to read. This is clearly my own personal experience, but when I've had readings from people face-to-face or on video, they want to explain to me that swords represent air, and this represents that, and I either agree with their technique and so know that already, or I don't agree with their technique and want to correct them. Either way, I'm not there to learn, I'm there for answers. And clients who aren't already readers don't necessarily know they're being taught, so they're listening to everything as they try to find out what their fate will be.

There's a common corporate aphorism, "If everything is important, nothing is important." This is as important to remember when you're doing readings face-to-face as when you're managing a project at the office. When doing a verbal reading, what you don't say is as important as what you do. And by that I mean, it's wise to edit yourself in real time.

Remember the aim of the reading: to answer the client's question. The bulk of what you express verbally should be toward that goal. The math of the reading should, as much as possible, remain silent. That's not easy to do. Partly because it involves choosing when to speak and when to be quiet—and that's a skill almost no human has mastered. Partly because silence is uncomfortable; partly because we want to get the answer out as soon as we can so that we don't freak our client out or seem like we don't know the answer.

This is why I recommend practice. Shocking, I know. I would recommend that you go back to the previous activity, and repeat it. Draw new cards for each, but answer the same questions. This time, speak them aloud. Try to only speak aloud the initial narrative and the final narrative. It's worth noting that what I'm asking you to do is somewhat unrealistic. That said, I'm still asking you to do it. Why? Because in practice we aim for idealism. It's more likely to lead to the clarity we seek than settling for "good enough."

I'm a stickler about this, despite my own failings with it, for reasons I've already stated: readings should be useful. And the point of this course is to take us closer to useful readings. When we fill spoken readings with all the math, remember that the client is taking note of everything as though it were all equally important. What they retain will be entirely out of our control, and so the less we can say that's not important, and the more we can say that is, the closer we get to giving useful readings, because the client doesn't have to sift through all the words we used in order to get to the final point.

It's not easy, but it's not supposed to be. If it were easy, we'd be doing it already.

NARRATIVES IN LONGER SPREADS

For the sake of example, let's explore how to handle narrative in larger spreads. I've already expressed my love for the nine-card grid. It's versatile, it's detailed, and it's useful as heck. It also happens to be a series of six three-card readings—which means you're well on you're way to creating narrative. We can get tripped up, and I have frequently been victim of this, in creating the narrative, but never weaving together the moral of the story. And morals are a useful thing to think of, here.

Remember Aesop's fables: a story with a lesson at the end. The story set us up; the lesson took the story and made it into a teaching moment. The story made the lesson memorable and interesting; the lesson made the story more valuable than just another tale.

Longer readings, regardless of the chosen spread, are fables: a story and a moral, a lesson.

Here's an example, and then you get to work:

Question: My husband and I have been together for eight years, and we love each other—but it feels like we're roommates a lot of the time. What's wrong with my relationship?

Cards drawn:

Narrative: Row 1 (theme of the reading): Hot and heavy passion (ace) wanes (two reversed)[1] when people don't spend enough time apart.[2]

Now, I'm going to read the rest of the rows and columns of three to explore the other narratives. I want to pay special attention to rows and columns that seem to validate my theme—or that contradict it outright. Both of those will be helpful when it comes time to create the moral of the story.

Row 2: Things change (wheel) when we've finished our work for the day (Ten of Coins) and we let emotional growth take a back seat (Three of Coins reversed).[3]

Row 3: Anxiety (Nine of Swords) makes you go off on intellectual rides (Knight reversed) that pull you deeper into your own mind—and away from the physical (Two of Swords).[4]

....

1   I'm playing fast-and-loose, here. The two means duality, expansion, partnering, pairing. Reversed would mess with that. The threes are about growth, and so a reversed three would suggest diminishment, or waning. But: a two reversed makes me think of going backwards, so in this case I just followed my gut—it felt like the passion that should be expanding is actually contracting, by moving backwards rather than forwards.

2   Playing a little fast-and-loose, again. The Hermit reversed says, "You're not spending enough time alone," to me. Especially in this case. Right out of the gate, I feel like "absence makes the heart grow fonder."

3   A confusing paragraph, so let me explain: The wheel suggests changing, that part is easy. I look at coins in part as duties or responsibilities and ten as completion—so it's like finished duties, or finished work. The Three of Cups upright would suggest emotional growth, but reversed I'm reading it as "taking a back seat" - not giving it the attention it needs and requires. So the initial passions of the first row have changed, in part because the emotional work of the relationship has turned into a duty or responsibility, not an act of feeling.

4   A row of swords suggests intellectualizing everything, for sure. But starting

Column 1: Passion (ace) changing (wheel) causes anxiety (Nine of Swords).[5]

Column 2: Being pulled between duty and excitement (Two of Wands reversed; Ten of Coins) leaves you fantasizing about how different things could be (knight).[6]

Column 3: Not enough time alone diminishes your feelings of growth and that leaves you of two minds about the relationship.[7]

All right, so now I have six narratives—or really an initial narrative, and

with the Nine of Swords as anxiety, the Knight of Swords reversed representing the person who asked for the reading (upright would indicate the other half of the relationship)—and the knight is a hunter. He's going off and doing his thing. So, s/he's thinking and going down these anxious paths. The Two of Swords suggests being pulled in two directions—it can mean being of two minds about something, which would be apt here. But in a reading about a relationship, I feel like there's a deficit of earth, water, and fire in this row—so I take "pulled" as being pulled deeper into the mind, where things need a more emotional and passionate approach.

5   I.e., the client is anxious because relationships start out sexy and passionate, but that changes.

6   I'm really going rogue, here. I use the Two of Wands reversed to represent both being pulled, and the idea of passion. I partner it with the Ten of Coins to represent duty. Because the Knight of Swords represents the mind, I'm suggesting that they're going on mental journeys—fantasies. Why am I doing this? Because it makes sense and it struck me as I looked at the cards. I'm not fighting that. Also, because I now have enough evidence to validate my claims, I'm "twisting" the meanings a bit to support that. Since this isn't a science, I can do that. I'm trying to prove my initial point. I'm not manipulating things so much that they're unrecognizable, but I'm taking pieces of the cards, parts of the whole, and letting them speak a narrative to me that supports my thesis. That is, I think, what Dr. Elias means when she says that cards don't have meanings.

7   Try to figure out how I got there yourself. I've definitely left clues in my footnotes.

five sub-narratives that either support or contradict my initial narrative, however you want to look at it. Now I craft that into a summary narrative that gives me the overall story. Here's what I might say (note that I'm not necessarily using my six narratives in the order I found them—I want to try to create a narrative that paints a picture of the relationship, not stay married to the six little scenes I created):

We're[8] feeling anxious in part, because relationships change from passionate to more banal. That's natural. Relationships do that, and luckily there are cycles to relationships. That lack of passion may have to do with the fact that you don't spend much time apart from each other, and that we start to treat relationships like duties, not emotional experiences. Nothing breeds contempt like familiarity; nothing kills passion more than duty. When that anxiety kicks in, we retreat into our mind, and fantasize about all the things that could go wrong—or that could go differently, anyway. We're caught between this mental world—and the more physical one around you, that could ground you. Intellectualizing everything is actually making the anxiety worse, not better.

---

8   Note that I use the word "we" a lot. That's a choice I sometimes make, especially if I've got something negative to say about the behavior of the client, or if the "fault" seems to lie with the client. In this reading, the partner doesn't really show up. They may be feeling equally as dispassionate, or they may be feeling fine. The only court card that shows up is the Knight of Swords, and, being reversed, that gives me a picture of the *client*. I don't have a sense of the other half of this relationship. That suggests the real issues belong to the person I'm reading for. I'm saying "we" so that I don't attack or implicate the client. Sometimes that can stop the client from shutting down. Sometimes it lets them off the hook. You have to use your judgment and decide what's best—but, word choice does matter.

What I've done here is taken a little bit, and woven the strands (the rows and columns) into something that tells a story, but is a little bit more coherent than the individual strands. I've painted a picture of the client's experience in the relationship.

Note, too, that I've woven a cogent narrative. Yay me! Time to end the reading!

No, it's not! But too many readings end here. The client didn't ask me what their relationship looks like, they asked me, "What's wrong with my relationship?" There are answers in that story, but I haven't highlighted them yet so that the client walks away with the answer to the question they asked. And this is where I have to be brutal with myself: I have to check in and ask myself whether or not I actually gave them what they asked for.

This is another reason I like written readings, because I can actually check my own work. In the heat of a spoken reading, I don't always remember what I said. Having a trail of breadcrumbs to follow is helpful. Again, though, that's my preference; it's not the law of the land. If I try to remain present and in the moment during a spoken reading, I can retain more of what I say in order to summarize.

Now, let me take my narrative and craft an answer to the question that I was asked:

There's nothing wrong with your relationship. You're going through the normal cycles that couples go through. What starts out as sexy and passionate eventually turns into something more daily and banal. Luckily, that is cyclical, and you won't always feel that way.

You may not be helping yourself, though, because of your anxiety about the situation. You're using that to fuel your mind with all kinds of fantasies about what should be different and what could go wrong. That's making things worse. Try not to intellectualize your relationship. You're using your mind, when this is calling for your body. It's not about thoughts; it's about feelings.

You may also just be spending too much time together. You may want to "miss" each other a little bit, so that you're not taking each other for granted. That's where most relationships get stuck.

Now I've woven all the strands I needed together into an answer to the question I was asked. It's not dramatically different from the version above it, but I've phrased my answer carefully around the question. "What's wrong with my relationship?" Nothing—except life.

Activity 9.2: Spread it out

Instructions: Answer the following question using a nine-card spread, using a similar series of steps to the ones I outlined above. Write it out, or—if you prefer—speak it into a recorder, so that you can listen to it again later.

Question: Every time I start a relationship it seems like it's going well for about two months, and then suddenly it just dissolves. What's going on? Why does this keep happening?

Debrief: Bottom line—giving yourself a system of interpretation can help you make sense of larger readings, and can give you more direction. Sometimes with larger spreads, the sheer amount of information can be overwhelming. Trying to mention all the nuances can overwhelm the client. If you take a slightly more systematic approach, you can drill down to the answer and leave them with a "moral" or answer that suits their needs—but also allows you the opportunity to explore everything the reading has to offer.

SHORT ANSWERS

Not every reading requires narrative. In fact, sometimes that level of detail can muddy the water. One of the things that set me down the path that eventually led to the text you have in front of you was the idea that tarot was more convoluted and vague than, say, Lenormand cards. Nonsense. I've seen people do perfectly cogent tarot readings, and insanely convoluted Lenormand readings. The medium is less important than the reader.

I've discussed at length that tarot has been spiritualized to within an inch of its life—and there is nothing wrong with that. But as above, so below (to borrow a phrase). Tarot can be used for path working, shadow work, life work, Kabbalah, Alchemy, meditation, and any number of other spiritual tasks—and it can also answer a damn yes or no question. It takes setting the intention and making an agreement with the cards before the reading. In this section, we'll explore two kinds of shorter-answer types of questions, and how you may go about answering them. These are closed (yes/no) questions and timing questions.

Closed (Yes/No) Questions

Yes or no questions are among the most common. "Will X happen?" I will answer them, as you now know, but I answer those particular kinds of question with a caveat. Here's a story to illustrate why:

Recently, my company was considering me for a promotion. It was an unusual situation, though, because I'd accepted a new role within the company only five months earlier. There is, at my level, a year-long waiting period before employees are allowed to apply for anything new. I was an extenuating circumstance, however, due to the nature of the job I'd had before and the conditions under which I'd arrived in my current role. Out of the gate, it felt unlikely that I would get the job—I'd already been promoted once that year, twice seemed impossible. Still, I did a three-card reading for myself on the question, "Could I actually get this job?" A yes or no answer. Using the system I'll describe shortly, I got a positive answer—yes, I could actually get this job. I hedged my bets: "Will I get this job?" The cards answered in the affirmative. I polished up my resume and wrote an unusually confident cover letter and clicked "submit" on the job website.

Following my first interview, I did a follow-up reading: "Will I get this job?" This time, I got a *maybe*. I had a coins card (indicating potential yes), a reversed Emperor (majors, as you'll see, can enhance a meaning), and the Knight of Swords (a swords card indicates a no). What I gathered from this spread was that it was a "maybe," but because the Emperor—the holder of the power, essentially—was looking at the "yes" card, they were leaning in my direction.

My second interview did not go well, by my estimation. One of the panelists was in the middle of a large meeting and couldn't hear everything I was saying, the other could hear perfectly—but the questions were unexpected, and I don't think I answered them well. Following that interview, I did a reading: "Will I get the job?" A spread of swords and wands—a definitive "no." It was as I thought. I had bungled my interview and ruined my chances. And as the days went by without a response—a whole week, in fact—I settled into the reality that while my first interview was as good as I'm capable of, I hadn't done well enough in the second interview to tip the other decision makers (in this case, whoever was represented by the Knight in that "maybe" spread) to my side. A few more days went by, and I did another reading—and I got another mixed spread—a maybe. Interesting. But I hadn't heard anything, and I knew the hiring manager wanted a decision set five days earlier. Clearly, this yes/no business did not work in tarot—and/or, I'm a horrible reader and should give up.

That evening, I got an appointment for a third interview. And another for a fourth. I did not do readings, because at this point I felt like I'd already lost the opportunity and these were pity interviews. With nothing to lose, I approached them without the apprehension of someone trying to be impressive. I asked the interviewer what her challenges were on her team, and I found myself saying, "Let me tell you how I can address those." I was exceptionally confident for a guy who spends most of the time feeling like he has to apologize for taking up space in almost every situation. A few more days went by; I avoided reading. And after a few more days, I got an offer for the job.

It a was a whirlwind, and it was made windier by the readings I'd done for myself. Did I do the right thing in attempting to predict my hiring? Were the yes/no questions I asked of the cards foolish? Should I have gone with the more common modern tarot question, "What can I do to improve my chances?" The answers to all of those questions are more complicated than a simple yes or no—and so is life.

Here is what I've taken away from that. In terms of rephrasing my question to, "What could I do to improve my chances?" I really knew the answer to that question. And, in a manner of speaking, I'd asked it in another reading: "What's the best thing to focus my answers on during the interview?" Three coins cards told me to focus on the practical application of my skills. But clearly I wasn't satisfied with just that answer, or I wouldn't have gone right to the money shot in, "Will I get the job?" And the definitive "yesses" I got from the early two readings allowed me to write a cover letter that was far more confident than I usually allow myself to be. I don't think that level of confidence hurt me, in this case. Now, had I allowed myself to get arrogant, that would absolutely have hurt my chances, which is the risk of asking this type of predictive question. And, had the reading said "no," I might not have applied, or gone in like a sad puppy and been unimpressive. That was a risk, too. But I knew that. In my case, the risk paid off, because it improved my confidence enough to write a convincing cover letter and do a first interview that, by my humble standards, was a home run.

What, then, about the intervening "maybe" and the definitive "noes" that followed? Therein lies the *real* risk in answering yes/no questions. Conditions change. I'm a believer that few things in life are absolutely set in stone. And when we read, we're reading the conditions at a given moment. A tarot reading is a candid snapshot of the energy around an issue at any given time. But as soon as that snapshot is developed, conditions might change—in the same way that the light changes during an outdoor photoshoot.

Looking at my experience over the course of this interview process was important, because it reminded me about that very fact. It's possible one or all of my readings were inaccurate, and that my getting the job was pure coincidence. It's possible, but doubtful, that I never had any competition and the job was mine for the taking. What is more likely, though, is that the conditions changed. I believe it was incredibly possible at the start of this process that I was a strong candidate from the point of view of the hiring manager , and I believe I stood a strong chance of getting the job. I further think that my poor performance at my second interview may have sown doubt in the minds of the additional interview panelists. I think that doubt may have affected some of the folks whose lives would be affected by the hiring, and they protested my candidacy. For several days—about a week, or so—I believe that I had been effectively knocked out of the running. And then I think conditions changed again, and I regained my status as a contender.

In *fact:* what I haven't told you is that the interviewer of my third (the unexpected one that came after a week or more or silence) told me that she had been upset that a candidate was going to be offered a position without her having the chance to talk to the candidates first, because she works closely with the person in the role. So now I know for a fact that someone was actively against my hiring—at least temporarily. That may well have been the energy in those negative snapshots I saw in the spreads. And it's possible, had I not been oddly confident in that third interview, I would not have won her over. And it's possible that I would not have been that unusually sure of myself had I not felt already like there was nothing to lose in being my most self-possessed.

This is all part of the tricky doings of "fate." Who knows whether anything I've gathered from this experience is true or whether it's nonsense. That's one of the frustrating things about being alive, and that's one of the reasons we want divination to guide us. We can't ever know for sure. And lord knows I've been wrong in predictive readings as often as I've been right.

This is all by way of saying that closed (yes/no) questions are tricky to answer, and having experienced what I've experienced, I'm now a believer in disclaimers when performing them for anyone. I share my philosophy around them (more concisely than I have here), and I express the nature of change. I do my best to ensure the querent understands that the answer is based on the conditions at work *right now*, and that conditions could change. In fact, the reading itself could have an affect on the outcome, because, as quantum physics tells us, the act of observing something changes it. All I need for evidence of that in tarot readings comes from the story I just told you: the initial positive readings gave me the confidence to throw my hat in the ring; the definitive no answers allowed me to approach an interview with a "nothing-to-lose" self confidence that is *not* my normal state. Once I clear my consciousness around the impact of closed question readings, I draw the cards and tell them what the snapshot says.

Wherever possible, I try to focus on "why." I think that's helpful, too.

Yes, I believe yes/no questions can be answered. Yes, they can be left at that. But given the changeable nature of life, I prefer to get the yes/no and then explore why that answer may have come up. It adds the empowerment that, frankly, is sorely missing from old school cartomancy, while it still answers the question asked. Now, being able to explain "why" depends on the client's willingness to hear the answer. That's not a lock, by the way. Because the psychological reaction in the brain will likely stop them listening, either way. If they get the answer they want, they're celebrating and picking out the furniture for their new corner office; if the answer is no, they're depressed and wondering why life is so unfair. Still, offering an explanation can be empowering *if* we manage to hold their attention after the initial yes or no. In the examples and exercises below, I explore simple short yes/no answers, but any of the techniques used throughout this book can help you add meaning. For example, consider the three-card yes/no reading I did that gave me a "maybe." I got the maybe from the combo of cards, but I got *why* it was a maybe by using the visual language (the Emperor was looking at the "yes" card, and not the annoying naysayer who wanted his attention).

Old school cartomancy is full of techniques that allow for yes/no answers. One might, for example, say that a three-card spread with a majority of wands and swords means "no," and a majority of cups and coins means "yes." Simple. What of a reading with three trumps? Well, what do you think? Odd numbers = no; even, yes? A majority of traditionally shadow cards (Hanged Man, Death, Devil, Tower, Moon) = no; a majority of traditionally light cards (basically everything else) = yes? Here's the thing:

you just make the choice. And you decide before you shuffle the cards. And you follow through with that choice as you conduct the reading.

Reading is all about intention and agreement. Remember that you are in charge of the cards. They're good assistants. They want to help you, and they will respond (usually)[9] to the agreement made. So just decide.

Let's look at some examples.

A client wants to know whether or not she and her ex will get back together again. It's a common question. Let's say I draw: Moon, Two of Cups, Ten of Coins.

I could go into a long story about how she's only seeing a fantasy version (Moon) of how she feels about her connection with this guy (Two of Cups), and that she'll finally find a more practical view (Ten of Coins) of the relationship.

Or, I could actually answer the question she asked me.

So before I shuffle I decide this:

Cups and Coins = yes

Wands and Swords = no

Trumps = an emphasis of the message, meaning that if I see a trump in the reading it adds exclamation points, italics, neon lights, and arrows to the overall message.

Trump + one yes card + one no card = the situation isn't formed enough yet to make a final determination.

....

9 I make agreements with the cards and *sometimes* they decide to flout those agreements. For example, I'll use my *reversed court = client/upright = someone else* agreement. There are still times when I look at the spread and think, "yeah, OK—that reversed Queen is actually someone else." I go with it. But that's because tarot is a fickle lover and I'm into that.

In this case, then, Moon + Two of Cups + Ten of Coins essentially says: *Hell yeah, you'll get back together girl! It's a lock!*

In such a case, the meanings of the cards don't actually serve any purpose. But, if I decide to agree ahead of time that the meanings of the cards will provide supporting documentation, as it were, I could do that. It's all in the intention I set.

Activity 9.3: Agreements

Instructions, Part 1: Create an agreement meant to answer each of the questions below, and then use a three-five card spread to answer the question. (I recommend odd-numbered readings because it's less likely it will end in a "tie.")

1. Will Don and I have children?
   a. Agreement:

   b. Cards drawn:

   c. Answer:

2. Will I get the promotion I was promised last year?

    a. Agreement:

    b. Cards drawn:

    c. Answer:

3. If I take this new job, will my family be OK?

    a. Agreement:

    b. Cards drawn:

    c. Answer:

4. Can I afford a new car?

    a. Agreement:

    b. Cards drawn:

    c. Answer:

5. I want to know whether I should keep seeing Mike.

   a. Agreement:

   b. Cards drawn:

   c. Answer:

Instructions, Part 2: Take it to the streets. Ask some friends or relations, if you can, if you can do a short-answer reading for them. You can use the ones above as examples. Perform the reading for real, and journal it. Then follow up with the friend to see whether or not the reading reflected what eventually happened.

   It's important to recognize that this is not a test of your skill. It's a gauge of whether or not these are the kinds of readings you want to do, or have any aptitude for. Generally, if you don't want to do them, your aptitude for them will be low. If you do want to do them, it may take practice, but you'll likely get there. To return to our friend Bob Ross, of the land of happy trees, talent is nothing more than applied interest. If you want to find a way, you likely will.

Debrief: Candidly, I bristle when I hear folks describe other forms of divination as more practical than tarot. Tarot is what we've made it, and other systems are what we've made them. No governing board decided that Lenormand or Sibilla must tackle practical matters, while tarot must remain ephemeral and nebulous. I've no interest in defaming Lenormand or its devoted and talented readers. I wish I could manage to read well with those cards. They don't resonate with me. Tarot does. The reason could be manifold, but I could throw my hands up in despair and say *I'll never be a practical reader who can answer questions about daily life!* Or, I can sit down and make an agreement with the cards, stick to it, and do my math. The same goes for you. All systems are as practical as we choose to make them.

Timing Questions

The other common questions are time-based—"when" questions. "When will X happen?" These are equally interesting, because they're frequently phrased in such a way that assumes the event will happen at all. "When will I get my promotion?" assumes that you are actually going to get a promotion. "When will the house sell?" assumes it's *going* to sell.

From my point of view, these are the most difficult to answer, because what the client wants is a day, date, and time: "You will sell the house on December 4th at 10:04 a.m. It will be sunny and clear, and you will suddenly find all your lifelong dreams have come true."

While I feel like tarot can be specific, I don't think it can be *that* specific. I also believe tarot tends to prefer *conditional answers.* By this, I mean that tarot seems best at telling us the conditions under which an event may happen, rather than the date or time of its occurrence. That's not to say it can't give us a sense of the time of year, but doing so means assigning timing meanings to the cards. For example, each of the suits represents a season (correspondences vary, so I say choose what draws you), and the card numbers could suggest a day, date or time. Like everything else, it comes down to agreement. There are books and chapters of books on this, but it's not something I practice, so I'm not going to explore it here.

You could also choose a spread that is literally a date spread. Three positions: position one representing the month, position two representing the day, position three representing the year. Doing so requires some creativity, but it is possible. Let's say, for example, I remove all the trumps from the deck, and choose the ten cards representing the last two numbers of the next ten years—up to twenty-one. This allows me to discover a year up to 2021. For anything beyond that, I need to get creative. Add the trumps one through ten to the numbers seventeen (the year of this writing) to twenty-one. So, for example, World (twenty-one) + Wheel (ten) = 2031. Next, I decide that pages equal eleven; knights, twelve; queens, thirteen; kings, fourteen. For the moment, though, I remove all the queens and kings, because we only have twelve months. So I shuffle the ace through the knight (twelve) of every suit and choose the month. Then, I return to the queens and kings and decide that I will draw three cards to represent the day of the month. I will add the three numbers together, and provided that it does not exceed thirty or thirty-one (depending on the month), I will use that as the day. If it does exceed the last day of the month, I will further reduce the number by adding the individual numerals together, and *that* number will be the day of the month. Then, I have my date.

For example, a client asks, "When will I meet my true love?"

I shuffle my trumps and draw the Moon (eighteen), so I have my year – 2018.

I remove the kings and queens from the minors, shuffle them for the month, and draw the Ten of Coins, reversed. In this case, the suit and reversal mean nothing—I need only the number. I now know that it will be October of 2018. Next, I return the kings and queens to the minors and draw the Ten of Cups, the Knight of Coins, and the Ace of Swords. That is ten + twelve + one, which equals twenty-three. Because that is less than thirty-one (the number of days in the month of October), I am done. My client will meet their true love on October 23rd, 2018! He lives happily ever after, and I quit my job and go on a tour of the talk show circuit exhibiting my incredible new skill.

Would I actually do that reading? Not as anything more than a parlor trick. And even then, probably not. Why? It assumes too much: it assumes there's such a thing as "true love," it assumes that my client is going to meet a true love (and that nothing is going to happen to either person in the meantime—such as meeting someone who they don't think is perfect, but that they're willing to settle for), and it assumes that I am capable of a level of predictive specificity not even fakers of Nostradamus couplets attempt to achieve. Also, think back to my interlude on being right. Suppose I predicted something with that level of precision and I was right. I'm not sure I would want to live with that power. I would be tempted, after a night of too much gin and too many ghost stories, to predict the date of my death—and then spend every second between now and that moment terrified. No. Better to live some with sanity and "settle" for a bit more of the unknown. Finally, I don't think there's a shot in hell I could do that trick and actually be right. And I don't really want to find out whether or not I actually I am.

This is one of the only areas of reading where I encourage clients to consider the limitless variables affecting predictive specificity. Anyone who has tried to sell a house, or knows somebody who has, can tell you that. You think you're about to sign the papers, and suddenly there are cracks in the foundation nobody noticed, and it's back to square one.

When it comes to timing questions, I prefer the conditional answers I spoke of at the start of this section. By a conditional answer, I mean that the reading explores a series of experiences or conditions that will align in order to make something possible. So the answer to the question, "When will I meet my true love?" would look more like this—even using the three cards I used in the crazy date example, above: The Moon, the Ten of Coins reversed, the Ten of Cups, the Knight of Coins, and the Ace of Swords.

Given this combo, I would say that they will meet their true love when their practical outlook overcomes (Ten of Coins) their fantasies (Moon) of what romance is supposed to look like (Ten of Cups), and they're capable of hunting for someone who is dutiful (Knight of Coins) and lights up their mind (Ace of Swords).

Is that answer better than the exact time and date? I think so. Why? Well, it's not remotely as sexy as being able to predict the exact day, but it doesn't make any assumptions about the client's fate. It addresses some of the things that may be keeping him from engaging in a relationship (dramatic romantic fantasies), and grounds them in what they may want to be looking for (someone who is dutiful and sparks their intellec-

Reversed

tual interest, rather than just the romantic or physical). This shouldn't really be a surprise if you've read this far. You've likely detected that I have a pretty earthy view of what makes relationships tick, and you've likely noticed that I frequently read romance questions with an eye toward smashing dewy-eyed idealism. Relationships are far from perfection, and the ones that last frequently require a *lot* of work. Relationships are as much coins as they are cups, but too many people forget that. I am here to remind them of it, curmudgeonly as that may make me. But I think that's a better answer than a time and date that may or may not come true—in fact, it likely won't—because I'm addressing the conditions under which something could happen. I'm not assuming it will or won't. It has an air of the predictive, which will hopefully make the client happy, and it has a commitment to will and overcoming passive living, which makes me happy.

I recognize I'm contradicting some of what I've said in the previous pages. In timing questions, I'm equivocating a bit more—but I am not diverging from my commitment to answering the question asked as precisely and practically as I can. From my point of view, this answer is the most practical, because it demands of the client that they recognize their own agency. If I go through the process of giving them a date and a time, I've taken them out of the equation and chalked it up to fate. If I give them conditions under which something is likely to happen, I've covertly guided them to action.

How is this different from answering yes or no questions, and why will I say "yes or no" when that could equally disempower a client? It's frankly a matter of choice. I've chosen to do that, because it makes sense to me. And you'll hopefully note that I prefer *not* to answer yes or no questions, and that when I do I believe in specific disclaimers and an effort to explore *why* something may turn out in the way the cards predict. But I also believe that yes or no questions are easier to answer than "when" questions, because while conditions change around closed questions, it isn't assuming something will or won't happen. It's addressing likelihood, potential, which timing questions don't. "When will X happen?" holds at its core that it *will* happen *at some point*, it's just a matter of *when*. I don't think life works that way.

Ultimately, you must decide what you prefer and what you're willing to do. If you take my parlor trick of identifying the date and it works for you and you're comfortable doing that, go for it—as long as you're willing to accept that responsibility responsibly, more power to you. Either way, it's up to you to decide and to make the agreement with the cards before attempting to answer the question. Like the system I've adopted for answering closed questions, the method you use is somewhat arbitrary. It doesn't really matter what methodology you decide to use, as long as you decide to use it and try to remain relatively consistent in it.

A final issue to consider in terms of time, whether or not the question is specifically time-based, is how far in advance you're willing to forecast. For example, if someone asks, "Will I find a boyfriend?" and you decide to answer the question, is your answer looking into the indefinite future? Or are you looking at a year, or so? This is another agreement it's important to consider, both for your confidence in reading, but also for the sake of the client. If you ask, "Will my client ever get a boyfriend?" and the cards say "no," have you struck them a blow. If you ask, "Will my client get a boyfriend in the next six months," that's a much more palatable amount of time, no?

Personally, I tend to limit anything remotely predictive to three months. I don't even do year-ahead spreads, because I think there are too many variables. Think, for example, about the 2016 presidential election. Throughout the winter and summer leading up to the election, predictive readers forecasted a win for Hillary Clinton. Something happened at the last minute, and suddenly everything changed—and I've heard predictive readers marvel at watching that happen in real time. (YouTube creator and author Donnaleigh Delarosa has an incredible discussion of this on her channel.) So, where I do agree to forecast something, I agree only to look around three months, or so. That's my choice; you can make another. But I do encourage you to set a boundary in that regard, because not only will it help you get more specific, it will help your client see and hear your answer more readily and more clearly.

Rather than a practice activity in this section, I'm going to suggest that you take some time to answer the following questions and explore your own method for answering timing questions. You're not carving anything in stone. You can—and likely will—change your theories about this as time goes on. But having a moment and a space to codify what you believe about these kinds of questions and how you'll go about answering them will be useful.

1. How specific do I believe I can get when answering timing questions?

2. Am I interested in *conditional answers*, or do I prefer to attempt more specific calendar timing?
   a. If I'm committed to calendar timing, what agreement will I make in terms of timing and card meanings? (For example, how will I tell the season, month, day, year, etc.)
   b. If I'm committed to calendar timing, how will I address the issue of likelihood. If a client asks, "when will X happen?", how will I address the assumption that it *will* happen?
   c. How much do I care about accuracy in calendar predictions, and what response will I engage if I'm wrong?

3. What is a reasonable amount of time to forecast, when attempting predictive answers?

4. How much am I interested in empowering my clients to be active,

and how much am I interested in simply answering the question?

Whatever you decide to do in regards to timing questions—or any kind of question—there isn't ultimately a right or wrong, as long as your intent is generous and you aim not to harm people. If you're charging money for readings, you should check out the laws in your area about fortune telling. Bizarrely, some are still in existence, and, equally bizarrely, some of them still get enforced from time to time. But whatever you choose, make the agreement, and give that agreement thought so that you're sure about what you're offering. After that, do what you do, and do it as well as you can. That's the most any client can ask for.

Interlude 6:

On Doubt

(with thoughts on arrogance and perfectionism)

Maybe I'm a cynic, but I don't trust people who never suffer doubt. People who appear to be effortlessly good at everything drive me crazy. Doubt is human. In my experience, the feelings of doubt and nerves are indicators that someone cares about doing something well. The real problem isn't so much doubt; it's panic. Doubt is a moment of, "What if I mess this up?" Yes, it's partly ego. We want to look good to the people we're reading for, or, if that happens to be ourselves, we want to feel like we're good at this. Panic, on the other hand, is consuming and distracting. That is when we get into danger.

Years ago, I was taking the correspondence course through the Tarot School in New York. My admiration for the proprietors and educators of the school, Wald and Ruth Ann Amberstone, is boundless—so it's important not to read this as a critique of their methods. It's an exploration of doubt vs. panic. One of the activities involved using a reading method called "The Voice in the Card." A friend agreed to be my test case. Leading up to the reading, I experienced doubt that I would be able to make sense of the reading. As I've said, most of my reading experience had been delivering written readings. There's a certain comfort in that method, because you have time to suffer through reading if you need to without anyone seeing you sweat. Doing a face-to-face reading for a friend, using an experimental technique I'd never tried before made me doubt whether I'd be able to make it work.

I arrived at my friend's apartment, we had dinner and drinks, and I got to the reading. That's when panic set in. As we set about reading. As I stared at the card, I realized that I had no idea what the hell the reading was saying. I stared down at the card (this was a technique that required only one card), and tried to make sense of the meaning in the context of my friend's question. As the silent seconds passed, my sense of self diminished. I felt sweat break across my forehead, and my confidence break in half. After long minutes, I finally conceded that I had no idea what the fuck the reading meant, and that I probably should go back to the drawing board. I felt mortified. I was certain my friend thought I was an idiot, and felt cheated by the experience (although, I'm sure, that's not remotely how she felt—I'm sure she didn't care all that much). To compound my humiliation, during my coaching session, Wald did an amazing job demonstrating the technique to me, and wound up predicting a whole new life path (which, incidentally, prevented me from finishing the course).

The point, of course, is not how brilliant the Amberstones are, though they are, but rather how doubt became panic, and that panic crippled me. I have no interest in giving away the technique taught by the Amberstones in this reading—if you'd like to know, I recommend reading their books, taking their telecourses, and/or getting yourself involved in their correspondence course. But suppose for a second that we're using a technique described in this course. Suppose I was doing a reading for you on the question, "What can I do to improve my love life?" Suppose the technique was to use one card and only the visual language of the imagery to answer the question. Suppose I drew the Two of Wands.

The image itself means nothing to me. I sit there, sweating. I don't understand how two crossed sticks and a couple flowers can make any recommendation about your blasted love life. I allow my confusion to mount, and I question my worthlessness as a reader and as a human.

That sounds funny, but of course it's not. The reality is that in those moments of doubt, that's exactly what we're doing: negating our own worth.

The famous quote attributed to Sigmund Freud, "Sometimes a cigar is just a cigar," could come in handy, though. If you ask me what you could do to improve your love life, and I'm sitting and staring at a picture of crossed sticks, if I take it at face value, as two crossed sticks, I could easily associate it with the crossed sticks of a vampire hunter. At which point I could say, "It might be good to stop treating love like a vampire coming to suck the life out of you. You don't need to make a cross and keep it at bay. It's ain't gonna hurt. Let it in."

That's easier to say now, with the benefit of experience, distance, and an imaginary client. But what makes the fake reading different from the real one? In my opinion, only the pressure put on yourself to be right. There is no pressure in a fake reading; there's no one to impress or disappoint. In fact, I've done some of my most impressive interpretations for people who don't exist.

You might argue that it's easier to read for a fake person, because you don't have any real situations to deal with. Anything is possible, and a fake person can't tell you you're wrong. But in my experience, I've found that the limitless possibilities granted by a fake reading make it harder to contain. If anything is possible, *anything is possible*. That means the options are equally limitless, and it's harder to land somewhere that makes sense. I don't mind the constraints of a real reading, but I don't like the constraints of pressure. I don't like the idea of failing, of appearing untalented, or disappointing people. And that is what gets in the way. But the thing that takes me closer to "failing" (as though such a thing were actually possible in a reading—who is there to fail you? The Tarot grading institute?) is the very pressure of worrying about failing.

There are people in the world who will say to people who feel such anxiety, "Don't worry about it! Just do it!" Well, that's easier said than done. In fact, the kind of person who says that kind of thing is the kind of person who likely has no actual idea what it feels like to experience that level of anxiety. It's easy for them to say, "don't worry," because they don't worry. At least not about things like this. But if you do worry about things like this, then you can't not worry about them. If you could avoid worrying, you'd avoid worrying. That's not the solution.

I don't honestly know that there is an easy solution. You feel what you feel in the moment you feel it, and you don't have a whole lot of control over that. That said, what you can do is practice awareness of how you're feeling.

See, panic is incredibly sneaky. It's frequently working without you even knowing or recognizing that it's happening. You're going along, experiencing your day, reacting to anxiety—because you're used to reacting to it—and it's making you miserable because it can. You're so accustomed to it, you don't really pay a whole lot of attention to it. In fact, if you're anything like me, you probably take it out on yourself—blame yourself. As though it's your fault you feel worried or anxious about doing something badly. And then when the self-fulfilling prophecy comes true, and you do give a shitty reading because you're so concerned about it, you beat yourself up again. And the whole time, you've probably never once stopped to consider that panic was at work.

You are not your panic. That's the weird thing. Because it happens inside of us, it feels like it is us, and it feels like it's our fault. It's not. And it comes from a place of caring, but it doesn't care about you as much as you care about it. And while you can't overcome in—in fact, fighting it makes it rear its ugly head even more aggressively—you can become aware of it. And you can reassert your power.

My therapist of many years has reminded me often that we can't kill panic. When we have a panic attack, we can't stifle it. Panic, anxiety, whatever it is we're suffering, is a way of our body communicating something to us. It wants care, somehow. It's a part of us saying "I need attention! Hello! Care about me!" It's not unlike a child, and we know what a child acts like when it wants attention it's not getting.

Becoming aware of the anxiety or panic we're experiencing during a reading allows us to pause, recognize the existence of the experience, talk it down from its heightened state, and reassert our authority over our being. We can say to it, "OK, I see you there. You want to make sure we're doing this well. We're going to, OK? I'm in control of this. But I need you to relax, because you're making it harder for both of us." Rather than wrestling it into submission, we engage it, care for it, talk it down, and come back into our power. By so doing, we're also getting rid of something that's pulling focus from the work in front of us. It's a start.

Is it always going to work? No. Will we always have flawless readings? No. Will there be times we draw the cards and stare at them as though we've ever seen them before? Yes.

Is it the end of the world? No.

When this happens, I find that I'm frequently missing the most obvious thing. I'm looking for deeper meaning in the cards, when two crossed sticks mean, "Stop acting like a vampire hunter; love isn't a parasite." For example. And it's why we keep a toolbox of techniques we can use when we need them.

Here's the other thing. If you just don't know, that's OK. It doesn't mean you're a bad reader. It doesn't mean you have to give up something you love. It doesn't mean all your practice and effort has failed you. It doesn't mean you'll never get good at this, or that you'll never give a good reading again. It's just what it is.

We are humans. We have bad days. We have times when we're tired, when we haven't been taking care of our own emotional needs. When those times arise, it's incredibly difficult to take care of others. When those times arise, we need rest—we don't need to be out there trying to divine something. Sometimes we're going to have moods; sometimes we're not going to be in the mood to read.

A lot of new tarot readers feel like they're not worth their salt if they're not building a paid client base. That's nonsense. If you give readings to friends and loved ones, that doesn't make you less a reader than someone who is reading for money. The word "professional" is one of the most annoying in the English language. What it literally means, that you earn money for doing something, has been conflated with the idea of self-worth and skill. The idea that if you're *truly* good at something, you should make your living doing it is nonsense. It's a side effect of living in a capitalist society. And I get it. As much as I don't like capitalism, I like having stuff. I wish that weren't true, but it is. I wish I were above that. I'm not. I understand how we conflate worth with money. But as I type this, I can't think of a single person I've ever had contact with in the tarot community who makes a living solely from reading for other people. All of them have a day job of some kind.

You can read "professionally" for free. You can read like an amateur for money. I've had readings from people who have no business charging, but they do it.

I bring this up, because it can be one of the factors that grates at readers. There can be immense (generally self-imposed) pressure to read for others, and to take a fee for it. That can happen before one is "ready" (and I don't fully know what I mean by ready, other, I guess, than that one has the self-confidence to ask for a fee—but see those readers who do and have no business doing that). The pressure to "go pro," to be "impressive" enough to warrant a fee, can be brutal.

Further, sometimes people feel that they will have more confidence once they realize people are willing to fork over funds to get readings from them.

If you don't feel confident reading in low-stakes situations for people who love you and want you to be happy, I can guarantee you won't feel any more confident reading for people who don't give a damn about you and just handed you fifty bucks to find out why their son keeps slipping back into drug use.

I don't mean to sound coarse. What I mean to do is make like Cher, and slap you across the face and say, "Snap out of it!" Don't feel any pressure to be any kind of reader, or do any kind of thing. Just do the thing that makes you happy. And enjoy it. This should be enjoyable. This is an enjoyable practice. Don't add pressure to yourself by aiming for professionalism when all that means is nothing.

I've been reading for nearly 20 years. I have an Etsy shop. And when people come to it, they're usually people I know. And because I know them, I inevitably talk them out of paying me. One client who does pay me tried to convince me to raise my prices. I wound up convincing her I should probably lower them. Does that mean I'm a bad reader? No. It means I'm bad at business. But those two things aren't the same.

The whole point of this ramble is not to add unneeded pressure to your practice by pushing yourself to some imaginary benchmark that exists only because we feel as individuals that to be a "real" reader, we need to make it our job. Because even if you're amazing, and even if you deserve a triple-digit reading fee, and even if you open up your e-store or brick-and-morter shop, it doesn't mean you're going to be a success. Here's a hard fact: The market for tarot readers isn't anywhere near as large as it seems like it will be. And when people make money from it, it's generally because they've built up a client base over time, and it took a *long* time.

Now, let's address the other side of this coin.

Very shortly after I started reading, I realized I should be writing a book about tarot. Why? Because I wanted to, and because I'd learned so much about it! There was the part of me that was sweating all the insecurity issues I talked about above, then there was the other side of me that thought, "Clearly everyone in the community is going to want to know what I have to say about this topic! I mean, come on! I've been reading for six months."

I'm not making that up. I wanted to start writing a book about tarot shortly after starting. And then I read an article in a tarot forum about new readers who think they know everything about reading, and want everyone to know they're experts (remember the people on the subway in New York, yelling about how effortlessly they navigate the trains?). This person said words that struck me to the core and have stayed with me ever since: "There's no expert like a novice." Devastating.

What's it mean? Basically, that nobody thinks they know more about a topic than someone who just started learning about it. It's more common than you'd imagine. And it's not a terrible thing. It's born of youthful enthusiasm (whether that youth is measured in years or passion). But youthful enthusiasm can quickly turn to arrogance if we're not careful. And even if doesn't go that far, the pressure to be an expert can stop us from being a student when we most need to be.

And you know when we most need to be a student? *Our entire damn lives.*

That may be the adult learning specialist in me saying that, but it's true. The second we feel we know everything there is to know about something is the second we should probably think about giving it up. Experts, in my humble opinion, got that way because they never tired of exploring the things that fascinated them. Hacks generally are the people who read one book on a topic and decided they knew all there was to know. The greats keep learning, keep growing, and never settle for "good enough."

◊ Lesson 10: Permission ◊

When I set out to write this, I had no intention of writing a certain number of chapters or lessons. But that my closing notes land on number ten makes me happy. There's a numerological synchronicity that affirms that—for whatever reason, and however it happens—tarot actually works. The number of completing cycles, finished projects, and new beginnings is the number of my final lesson.[1]

Together, we've gotten in the dirt.

So many of us are concerned with how we look (physically, or otherwise), that it's difficult to crawl in anywhere and make a damn mess. One of my aims with this book was to do that together. To create a giant mud pit that we could play in, like happy piglets, and roll around in the messy

---

1   Yes, cynical Cindy, there are interludes and an appendix—but those are designed differently. So there.

business of getting better at something we love.

My sincere wish is that you've really gotten deep into that dirt—and that you're enjoying being there. And that you're committed to staying there.

The methods I've discussed aren't the only methods. My approach isn't the only approach, and to use it you don't have to sacrifice any other, more metaphysical approach. We've added another layer, a delicious, fertile, mud-colored layer. It smells like rain and patchouli and pine needles and campfire.

I hope you gave yourself permission to make a mess. To do practice readings that were weird and made no sense and that you had to sweat and wrestle with. I hope you dove into the deep end and tried your best to silence the inner critic that tells you you're not good enough, that you'll never do this as good as so-and-so, and that you should just go back to passive engagement in whatever life wants to throw at you.

I hope that you'll give yourself permission to continue on the journey. One trait I've noticed in creative people is the need for permission. From writers and painters to tarot readers, people who are interested in doing things that don't fit inside the standard, capitalist view of what is valuable seem to need the affirmation of someone else to tell them it's OK to keep doing it. It goes back to my thoughts on "professional" readers. If you're not making money doing it, then you're not a "pro." We need someone to grant us permission to do things we love. But nobody can give you that, because nobody has that power. You are the only one who can give you permission... unless... maybe the tarot can...

Activity 10.1: Permission Slip

Instructions: Perform a three-card reading for yourself with the question, "How do I know I have permission to do what I love?" Use the techniques we've learned together to answer this question in a way that grants you permission to keep doing this work that you love. Yes, you're going to manipulate the cards to give you affirmation. Yes, you have permission to do that. No, that permission doesn't come from me; it comes from the fact that we're working with 78 pieces of paper that somehow, someway manage to help us on our journey in life. It comes from the fact that, somewhere out there, we have exceptional magic that allows us to work with such things. And it comes from the fact that you want it to happen.

This may take some sweat. You way draw three cards and feel your heart sink in confusion. Sweat it out. Get muddy. Get dirty. Wait it out. Work it out. You will get there. You have permission for this not to be easy. You have permission for this to take a month or a year to get the answer. That permission doesn't come from me; it comes from you. Grant yourself that permission. You'll be glad you did.

Debrief: Tens aren't just the end of a cycle, they're the beginning of one. The combination of one and zero is incredible, because it is both ten and *1+0 = 1*. Meaning that this chapter returns us to the ace energy of seeds, possibilities, beginnings, potential, and all of those one-like terms we explored back in our earliest lessons. Except you're ace to a higher power, now. All of that seed-like potential is elevated, because you've learned new things; you've changed. You're not the reader—or the person—you were when you began this journey.

Learning professionals talk about transformation in very practical terms. The measure of success for a learning event in the world of training is based on transformation. At the end of a course I've written, I like to ask learners to pause and answer this question: What can I do now that I couldn't do before? I do that, because training that doesn't clearly answer that question isn't training. Or, anyway, it's failed training. Transformation is the most important part of the learning process. In the way that we are transformed by readings that are practical, useful, and clear. Tarot readings are, oddly, a form of cartomantic training. And so is the book you're holding now.

Activity 10.2: What Can I Do Now?

Instructions: Use the space below to answer the question, "What can I do now that I couldn't do before I started this course?" Don't use the cards for this. Use you. Use your experience. And use all the work you recorded in the activities in the previous nine lessons. Don't rush this. You may want to come back to it over the course of the next few days, weeks, and months. Each time you do a reading and you realize you've internalized a technique that you hadn't previously, record it here. Revisit this from time to time. And repeat this activity after every book you read, course you take, or YouTube video you watch. Because every time you do those things, you're a different reader than the one you were before you read, practiced, or watched. You are transformed every time you learn something new about something you're passionate about. And your passion is likely to stay *en fuego* as long as you keep learning new things about what you're passionate about. And every time you learn something new, ask yourself: "What can I do now that I couldn't do before?" And write it down. Because I said so. But also because you've granted yourself permission to be the best at this that you can be. You granted yourself that, and you deserve to follow it through.

Final Interlude:
◊ More thoughts on ◊
the Elements

We've spent a fair amount of time discussing the elements already. But one thing that I like to consider in readings is the way that the elements partner with one another.

In my early days of reading, I learned about "elemental dignities." The way I learned it, this meant the way elements were disposed toward one another. The active/masculine elements got along well; the receptive/feminine elements got along well. These were dignified toward one another. But the masculine and feminine elements were ill-dignified toward each other, which meant that the combination of them could cause trouble.

Despite the somewhat sexist overtones of this, it turned out to be useful in readings. In those days, my most used spread was a five-card layout in the shape of a star—as below.

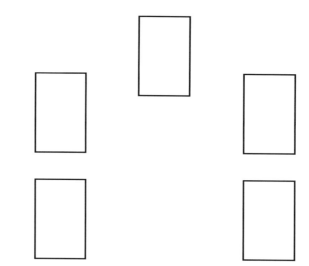

The top left represented fire, the top right represented air; the bottom right, water; the bottom left, earth. The tip was "spirit," and that was embodied by the major arcana suit. If, in a reading, a fire/wands card showed up in a cups/water spot, that indicated a conflict in that area of the client's life.

Over the years, I've developed a more nuanced interplay with the elements. Fire and water aren't always adversarial. Sure, water could put out fire; fire, evaporate water. But when they're working together, they create steam. That's a far more productive thing, especially if we're trying to get a motor going. If a client is asking about trying to make something happen, the combination of fire and water are a good thing—there's clearly enough fuel and energy to push through to the next phase.

Air is always a nebulous element. We've already talked about the ways it is frequently viewed as the most negative. Odd to me, because it's the thing every living being needs to survive. Water has air in it; nothing grows in and on the earth without it; and if there's no air, fire can't burn. If we have a combination of fire and air in a reading, and we're looking at whether or not something is sustainable, I would say that's a good sign. The air is providing oxygen for the fire to keep burning. An absence of air in this kind of reading would signal to me that it's likely to burn out pretty quickly. Readings with an absence of swords cards might suggest that someone is suffocating in a situation. On the other hand, readings with a lot of air could indicate that they're feeling dizzy from being over-oxygenated.

Water is romantic, and it can get anywhere it wants to. I think about *Memoirs of a Geisha*, and how Sayuri says that if water's path is blocked, it finds another way. Water can carry us along, and provide us a route of escape. But as I type this chapter, two huge hurricanes have demonstrated to the continent the destructive power of water. Readings overfull of water could suggest someone drowning in a situation. A reading about finances with a lot of water cards could suggest "drowning in debt." An overly watery reading might need some fire to help dry or evaporate that fluid; or some earth to give all that water something to soak into.

What about the generally even and grounded earth element? Earth, like air, feels somewhat neutral. But what of an absence of earth? Have you lost your roots, or a connection to the things that hold you down? Are you avoiding your duties or responsibilities? What about an over-abundance of earth? Are you buried in responsibilities, or are you in over your head?

Not much needs to be said about too much fire in a reading, but what about not having any? Are you too cool for school? Too apathetic? Where's your passion?

Looking only at the elements, not the card meanings or even the card images, consider what the following spreads might be telling you.

Example: Why am I so miserable at work?

Answer: All these cards have fire or air associated with them, in my mind (the Eight of Coins, the Magician and the Tower both have an implicit or explicit lightning involved with them). The air is fanning the flames. You're giving all the energy you have to your job, and you're not sustaining it or allowing for anything else.

Your turn:

1. I want this relationship to work. What could get in the way?

   Two of Cups, Lovers, Ten of Cups

   Answer:

2. My relationship is suffering, and I can't figure out why.

   Three of Wands, Ten of Swords, Two of Cups, Three of Coins

Answer:

3. I want to change careers. Why can't I figure out what I want to do?

    Three of Swords, Three of Wands, Five of Swords

    Answer:

4. I've always wanted to be an actor, but I never seem to make myself take the leap. What's going on what makes me avoid something I really want?

    Two of Cups, Three of Coins, Nine of Coins, Queen of Coins

Answer:

There aren't any right or wrongs, here. This is in a way a kind of "sub-text." Actors and directors talk about subtext a lot. It's the thing that isn't being said directly, but lies under what is being said. A great example of subtext is the word "interesting." Say you've created what you consider to be a brilliant work of art, and your friend says, "that's interesting." The subtext is essentially, "that's nice, but I don't like it and don't really care enough to tell you." Or at least that's how it frequently feels. (Something to consider, by the way, if you have creative friends.) Subtext isn't always negative. We use it when we're flirting. "I hate you!" could very well mean, "I love you, take your clothes off." The interplay of the elements could suggest a subtext to the reading. Take the first question, above. I gave you (deliberately) three traditionally positive cards, particularly in relationship readings. But I asked what would get in the way. If you were on board with my suggestions, above, you might have said something like, "you're over-romanticizing things!" Because you've got a lot of cups and the Lovers.

I chose that example specifically, because it's tempting when seeing a draw like that to say, "nothing could get in the way! This relationship is going to be everything you've ever wanted." Mmmm, yeah. That doesn't exist. And the aim is to answer the question that was asked. I guess it's possible that you could answer a question with "nothing." But there are few questions in life that really deserve an answer like that. So, if you really want to answer the question that was asked, you could use this technique. It's just something that's there for you, if you need.

It's now worth addressing the sheer number of tactics you could use. In this course alone, we've covered a whole host of things you could do to add shade and color to a reading. Great. But in the heat of a reading, attempting to do all of those things could lead you to mental paralysis. Sharing things like elemental dignities, or whatever you want to call what we've just explored together, is meant to give you helpful tools to reach for when you need to reach for something. Most of the time, I would say more often than not, what you need comes to you in the course of reading. If you need the elemental relationships we've explored, using them will occur to you. If it doesn't, it won't.

Having all the tools in your toolbox doesn't mean that you have to use them all, or that they even make sense for every application. The point is that you have them when you need them. And the nice thing about these kinds of tools, unlike a real toolbox, is that you can carry this one around without needing a truck—or a super strong back.

The key to being a good reader isn't using every tool in your arsenal; it's reaching for the right tool for the right job. You don't fix a clogged sink with a hammer.

◊ Appendix ◊

MUSINGS ON THE TRUMPS

The meanings I've developed for the cards evolve over time—and within the context of the reading I'm doing. But, for the sake of interest and if you're curious about how I arrived at some of the interpretations I did in the examples, here is a quick overview of the keywords I reach for most often with the trumps. Keep in mind that these are accurate as of the time I wrote this list. They've been developed from years of reading amazing books, years of doing readings—both amazing and not, and years of listening and watching and trying to connect the cards to the world outside. In the days, months, years to come, they will evolve even more. Nothing ever stays the same.

Trump	Light	Shadow
The Fool	Fearlessness, freshness, rough-and-ready willingness to jump in with both feet; innocence in search of experience.	Foolishness, recklessness, rash action, thoughtlessness, riskiness.
The Magician	Becoming a conduit of energy, pure creation; craftiness, wiliness, cleverness.	Errant energy, unfocused energy; fraud or dishonesty; hacking
The Papess/High Priestess	Gatekeepers, guardians, thresholds and goals—what we want to achieve that is achievable, just out of our reach. Teachers who make us work to get the answer.	Withholdings, snobbery, exclusivity; blockages, stoppages, what's unachievable, what's out of reach.
The Empress	Abundance of fertility, fecundity, potential for potential, receptivity/reception; nurturing, motherhood, mothering; earthiness, produce.	Barrenness or conversely over-abundance. Infertility, squandered potential, neglect; abuse, difficulty conceiving (of ideas and children), inability to produce—or, conversely, producing too much.
The Emperor	Sturdiness, solidity, command, power, surety, leadership, duty.	Conservatism, rigidity; weakness, or dictatorship; surety in what's wrong; dereliction of duty.
The Pope/Hierophant	Tradition, faith, traditional faiths; higher powers; religious leaders; devotion, meditation, prayer; institutions, especially longstanding ones.	Outmoded traditions, unhealthy or unhelpful beliefs; lack of faith, or, conversely, blind faith; inability to pray or meditate; faulty institutions.

The Lovers	Adult choices, weighing options, thoughtful selection; abundance of choices; instinct about what's right and wrong, and being able to choose right. (In Waite-Smith decks, I also look at this as seeing things as they *really* are, since the tree of the Knowledge of Good and Evil showed Adam and Eve a reality they couldn't see before—especially when paired with the Judgment card.)	Avoiding choices, or making childish choices; not having choices; knowing what's right and wrong and choosing what's wrong.
The Chariot	Masterfully bringing together opposing forces to create movement in the right direction; forward motion in general; Solomon-like problem-solving (remember cutting the baby in half)? The ability to resolve arguments or disputes equitably.	Stalled motion; inability to fight disputes, or, worse, make disputes more dramatic; inability to bring opposing forces together; foolish problem solving.
Justice	Balance, equity, equitable results; the right thing; objectivity; objective leadership, or generally true leadership; knowing that the just thing isn't always the "fair" thing; ethics.	Inequity, imbalance; not knowing right from wrong; bad leadership, or unethical leadership; doing what's "fair," when that's not what's right.

The Hermit	Solitude; mentorship; introversion; wisdom, study, asceticism; spirituality, especially those that are in contrast to the kinds of traditional spiritualties represented by the Pope; quiet, peace, inner guidance.	Reclusiveness, shut-ins; false prophets or gurus; teachers in it for the money, not the students; spending too much time alone, or not spending time wisely.
The Wheel	Cycles, shifting, changing, evolution, impermanence, adjustment; actual wheels; anything that turns, including worlds and stomachs.	Devolution, halted cycles; flat tires and stalled engines; real or metaphorical nausea; dizziness, real or imagined; or, spinning to fast, things changing too quickly, things seeming out of control.
The Hanged Man	Positive and/or necessary sacrifices; inward-turning; new points-of-view.	Punishment or consequences; avoiding sacrifices; refusing to see things in a different way.
13 (*La Mort*)	Gardening, harvest, or reaping what you sow (for better); autumn; ending, transition, transformation; finality; decisions; orgasms (which we called in Victorian times, "little deaths.")	Reaping what you sow (for worse); failed harvest, destroyed crops, drought; clinging to what's gone; mourning what hasn't been lost; winter; endless mourning; indecisiveness; things that just won't end.
Temperance	Moderation, temperance (literally); mixology or cooking; emulsification; blending, sharing; steady-handedness; portioning things out; carefulness; hydration	Immoderation or intemperance; shakiness; dehydration; carelessness; oil and water, or things that won't mix.

The Devil	Sex, particularly of the kinky and/or rough variety; theatre, playfulness, play-acting; connection to darker (but still healthy) aspects of life; animals; playing "devil's advocate"; indulgence, in a good way; letting go, in a good way.	Abuse, bondage; over-indulgence; feeling or being trapped; addiction; deceit; gambling; working with things that you don't fully understand the danger or impact of; sleeping with the enemy; selling your soul to get what you want.
The Tower	Orgasm, especially ejaculation; sexuality in general; swift change, clearing away the dreck or bad habits; cleaning house (in a good way).	Explosions of all kinds, but especially disagreements, blow-ups, and fights; things changing too soon; things changing too much; destruction; debris.
The Star	Direction, navigation; hope; gentleness, softness, quietude, peacefulness; the calm after the storm.	Directionless, unable to navigate; lack of hope (not hopeless, though); boredom.
The Moon	Fantasy, instinct, intuition; flattering light; seeing in the dark; seeing what others can't; nighttime.	Unreality, or living in a fantasy world; acting like an animal (in a bad way); inability to see; not seeing what others can see.
The Sun	Brightness, light, day; happiness, joy, success; brilliance or even genius; warmth; siblinghood; energy, enthusiasm.	Burnt or burning or too bright to see; overly enthusiastic; braggadocio; hot, humid, sticky; no shade, no rain.
Judgment	Wake up calls, realizations, revelations; communication, phone calls or e-mail; news; volume; exercise; up and at 'em.	Much the same, but of less shadowy things; lack of communication; oversleeping; denial.

The World	The world, literally—and so, travel; completion; wholeness; exuberance; the kind of change that comes after a major life lesson; size, breadth, depth; completeness; all good things.	Most people don't associate any shadow with this card. One might say all of the things to the left, but to a slightly calmer degree. You could also say that it's a dream deferred for a while.

REVERALS WITH MARSEILLE DECKS

If I use reversals with a Marseille deck, in which many of the pips are symmetrical, I mark the bottom right corner with a dot so I can tell if it's reversed.

SPREADS

What's a tarot book without a list of great spreads? Well, I've already given you the ones I use most. Everything for me is a multiple of three, and so I'll do spreads of three, six (sometimes, but rarely), and nine (all the damn time). These are useful for most occasions. There are spreads that I've used a lot that come from other writers, and so I won't repeat them here. But I can heartily recommend Camelia Elias's "Council of Thirteen" and the line-spread in J-M David's book.

Ultimately, though, the spread is just another agreement that you make with the cards before you shuffle and lay them out. It doesn't matter as much what spread you choose, as that you have an understanding of what you're asking the spread to do at the start. Make sure that the positions you choose are going to help you *answer the question that was asked.*

One of the main reasons I'm always shocked by the popularity of the

Celtic Cross is not that it's not a fine spread, but it doesn't seem to answer the kinds of questions that most people seem to ask. It actually seems to answer ten different questions, or maybe a smaller subset of related questions. But in terms of answering *a question*, it doesn't do much. Though Arthur Rosengarten Ph.D., does have a great adaptation of this spread in his book, *Tarot and Psychology: Spectrums of Possibility.* Again, nothing against the CC spread. But if you're going to use it, make sure it answers the question you're asking.

If a client asks whether or not their partner is cheating on them, a *past, present, future* spread is unlikely to answer that question. Well, except for the middle card, which explains that's going on now. So get rid of the past and future, and focus on the present. Likewise, if the client asks, "Will I sell this house?" Past, present, future? No. Future. And don't even think of giving me a *mind, body, spirit* spread if I ask you that!

If I ask you for a general reading, the five-pointed star spread—in which each card represents an element, and each element a part of life—might be a great option. But not if I say, "What do I do about this promotion I want?"

This may seem to some like a pretty obvious point, but I'm surprised by how many people a) use the same spreads for readings, regardless of whether or not it makes sense; and b) don't know that they have the freedom to make up a spread for any and every question.

To paraphrase Hamlet, suit the spread to the question, the question to the cards, and the cards to the answer. Beyond that, make up or use any spread you want! Give yourself that permission.

RECOMMENDED READING

Throughout this course, I've quoted books and sources whose work I admire. Here is a list of books referenced within, or that are generally great resources.

Reading the Marseille Tarot, by Jean-Michel David. Published by ATS (Association for Tarot Studies). Available through the author's website www.fourhares.com, or through lulu.com. This is a hefty book, and the print edition has an equally hefty price tag. But it's worth having the printed book, because you will want to write in it. The e-book is far less expensive, and is a printable PDF—but if you think you're going to save money printing it and getting it bound, you likely won't. Still, this is an exceptional course in Marseille tarot, and I learned some amazing things from it.

Marseille Tarot: Towards the Art of Reading, by Camelia Elias. Published by Eyecorner Press. Available from Amazon in print and e-book. The opposite of the prior book in every way. It is slim, brief, and terse. But, given the number of times I quoted Dr. Elias, here, you can see that it is equally impactful. Her reading style is specific, and likely not to everyone's taste, but she is absolutely a great teacher and whether you agree with her on every point, you'll learn something amazing. Her blog, https://taroflexions.wordpress.com, is equally excellent.

Tarot: The Open Reading self-published by the author, or *The Marseille Tarot Revealed*, published by Llewellyn. Both by Yoav Ben-Dov. This is the same book with two different titles. *The Open Reading* was published first and then Llewellyn republished and repackaged it posthumously as *The Marseille Tarot Revealed.* Both editions contain the same information, so it's really a matter of which you want to get your hands on. I have seen the latter in major chain bookstores, so it may be easier to find. But both are available online, and as e-books. Either way, it's an excellent book—especially in the numerology of cards. I recommend this as one of your references in the numerology activity in the pip chapters. Dr. Ben-Dov passed away not too long ago, but his website is still up and running, and contains images of his recreated version of the Conver Marseille deck—along with interviews, and a wealth of other information. http://www.cbdtarot.com

The Way of the Tarot: The Spiritual Teacher in the Cards, by Alejandro Jodorowsky. Published by Destiny Books. I find parts of this book as frustrating as anything that came out of the Golden Dawn, and while Jodorowsky is critical of Waite, he seems to use similar tactics in his book. That said, it's thorough, thoughtful, and numerologically it's helpful—and this is another source I recommend for that activity. It's also a big book with a lot of information, and many, many, many people love it.

Tarology, by Enrique Enriquez. Published by EyeCorner press. There is a documentary about this author with same name as the book. I recommend watching it before attempting to read this slim-but-dense text. Enriquez is a poet, a fan of wordplay, and a fan of visual rhymes. As such, what he has to say is fascinating—but can be interminable, if you don't have a sense of his style before going in. The documentary is available to stream on Amazon at the time of this writing, and I recommend it—not just because of the author, but also because of the many tarot names and faces that you will likely recognize and admire.

These next few are not related specifically to reading pip-style or Marseille decks, but are useful and were quoted herein:

Tarot: History, Symbolism, and Divination, by Robert M. Place. Published by Jeremy P. Tarcher/Penguin. Available at most large online booksellers, as well as smaller tarot-themed sellers. One of my all-time favorites. Mr. Place knows what he's talking about and talks about it in a fascinating way.

Seventy-Eight Degrees of Wisdom, by Rachel Pollack. Published by Weiser. Available at most large online booksellers, and any tarot-related bookseller. A classic for good reason. In fact, it's considered a crime not to recommend it—and for equally good reason.

A Wicked Pack of Cards, by Michael Dummet, Ronald Decker, and Thierry Depaulis. Published by Bristol Classic Press. Out of print, but not hard to find used—though it can be pricey, if you're not patient. This is history and nothing else, but does whet the appetite of anyone who wants to know the pre-Golden Dawn history of the cards.

The Esoteric Tarot, by Ronald Decker. Published by Quest Books. In some ways, a follow up to *Wicked Pack of Cards*, but with an esoteric bent. Decker argues that tarot was *always* esoteric. I'm not sure I agree, but his exploration of the history of divination is incredible, and he's a smart historian and tarotist with lots worth reading. Available at most online book retailers, and as an e-book.

The Tarot: History, Mystery, and Lore, by Cynthia Giles. Published by Fireside. A slim, fast read, but full of insight and information. Similar to Robert M. Place's book, but with a different tone, and an equal-but-distinct point of view. Available at online book retailers, and potentially some smaller tarot-related shops. I don't think this book gets enough attention.

The Tarot: Methods, Mastery, and More, by Cynthia Giles. Published by Fireside. Out of print, but not hard to find if you're patient. A follow up to the previous book, it's focused more on using the cards.

Professional Tarot, by Christine Jette. Published by Llewellyn. Available from online book sellers. A really great primer in everything a tarot reader needs to consider before taking the plunge into a money-making career—including how to close a business. Some of the information about the internet is slightly dated, but by-and-large the book remains as great as it was when it was published.

And then for Waite-Smith fans who have put up with all of my pipishness:

The Secret Language of Tarot, by Wald and Ruth Ann Amberstone. Published by Weiser. An incredible deep-dive into the symbolism used in Pamela Colman Smith's artwork. It's one of my favorite books on tarot.

The Complete Tarot Reader, by Teresa Michelsen. Published by Llewellyn. Out of print, but not an expensive purchase from sites that sell used books. This is a nice overall course on reading, and it addresses the concept of question really well.

RECOMMENDED WATCHING

In this day-and-age, much of the tarot world isn't writing books—or only writing books. They're on YouTube making videos. If you want to learn more about reading with pip cards or Marseille-style cards, I recommend Kelly Fitzgerald's YouTube channel (and blog) *The Truth in Story.* She's got playlists of tutorials on every kind of divination you can imagine, including Marseille-style and pip decks.

There are dozens, if not hundreds, of YouTube channels dedicated to the art of tarot, and it would be impossible to record them all there. First, I enjoy so many of them; second, such things come and go. In the name of not leaving anyone out, I'm choosing Kelly only—since she is in many ways, the Empress Card of the YouTube tarot community. But search YouTube for tarot, or attend one of Kelly's weekly live chats, and you will find channel upon channel to whet your tarot appetite.

Oh, you can also find me there, too. Search Tom Benjamin, and you'll find tutorials, tips, techniques, and enabling walk-throughs of decks I love.

RECOMMENDED DECKS

Marseille-style decks tend to be slightly pricier than Waite-Smith inspired decks. My guess is that this is in part because of the wider use of Waite-Smith inspired decks and that many pip-based decks are published and printed in Europe. That said, many are available and more become available each year. I think prices will drop as the popularity of these kinds of decks increase.

   If you're looking for one, here are some of my favorites. I've excluded anything I know to be out of print, though a dive into eBay's deep waters can usually yield amazing out of print options.

The Marshmallow Marseille by Wandering Oracle and featured in this volume. Available at www.wanderingoracle.com

The Tarot of Jean Noblet redrawn and reprinted by Jean Claude Flornoy. This is a recreation of what may be the earliest Marseille-style deck. Available from http://www.tarot-history.com/boutique/index.html

The Ancient Italian Tarot published by Lo Scarabeo. A reprinting of the Soprafino tarot from Italy. Beautiful and available at online booksellers.

Tarot of the Four Elements by Isha Lerner and Amy Eriksen. Published by Bear & Company. A beautiful, colorful, modern deck based on the kinds of elemental associations published here.

La Corte Dei Tarrochi by Anna Maria d'Onofrio, published by Il Meneghello. A one-of-a-kind tarot, published in limited editions by Italian tarot impressario, Osvaldo Menegazzi. Perhaps my favorite deck. Available from boutique tarot shops online.

The Wild Unknown by Kim Krans, published by HarperElixer (after earlier self-produced editions). One of the most popular decks of modern times, and a true beauty, it isn't strictly a pip-style deck. But it isn't *not* one, either. Popular enough now that it's available in online bookshops and many brick-and-morter shops.

The Pagan Otherworlds by Uusi. Another deck that straddles the world of pip decks and more situational decks. But the scenic elements on the pips aren't distracting to the eye. Available from https://uusi.us

Arcana Playing Card Tarot by Dead on Paper. Takes the standard 52 playing card deck, adds knaves, the trumps, and small suit symbols to the pips to make a unique and beautiful deck. Available at https://deadonpaper.myshopify.com

These are decks that I use frequently, but there are hundreds of others gracing the pages of major online booksellers as well as smaller online tarot shops. A couple of my favorite indie tarot sellers are:

The Tarot Garden: http://www.tarotgarden.com
CollecTarot: https://www.collectarot.com

And, internationally, TarotBG: http://tarotbg.eu/en/

Want more from this book?

Private coaching is available. I can work with you on your exercises or review your results and provide guidance or feedback. Contact me via my website. Folks who bought this book will get a discount on coaching lessons, so be sure to contact me for the current promotion code.

www.curiousjourneytarot.weebly.com

Photo by Chad Runyon

ABOUT THE AUTHOR

Tom Benjamin is the *nom de tarot* of playwright, instructional designer, and tarot reader Ben Jolivet. Ben has read tarot for more than 17 years, and has created content for his You Tube channel since 2012. He has won awards for both his stage plays and his instructional design, and loves helping people find their voice— whether in theatre, tarot, or corporate learning.

Printed in Great Britain
by Amazon